Hello It's Joe

JAMES D. PATALON

THE TWO JOES

AN UNAUTHORIZED FILMOGRAPHY OF THE LAST FILMS FEATURING THE 3 STOOGES

2

THE TWO JOES

BY: JAMES D. PATALON

THE TWO JOES

THE TWO JOES

BY: James D. Patalon

An unauthorized filmography of The Three Stooges with Moe, Larry and Joe Besser & Curly Joe Derita.

DEDICATED TO ALL THE JOE LOVERS!

About The Author: James D. Patalon was born in Detroit, Michigan. He currently resides in Nevada. He is a husband, father and grandfather. He works in retail.

To Emily
Best wishes
Joe Besser

Contents:

INTRODUCTION

This is the revised and reedited HELLO IT'S JOE. Looking over that book, I knew I had to fix some major errors from that particular piece of work. It was my first attempt at creating a unique Three Stooges Book. After receiving my proof, I realized the pictures as well as the actual format of the book was rather bad in the way it was handled and I believe that in order to appreciate the work done by the Stooges one must show a better respect for their particular form of comedy art.

I initially choose this subject because I was tired of all the supposed Three Stooges fans out there that considered Joe Besser a non-stooge. They continually have compared him to both Curly and Shemp Howard who came before. I think it is above time that both Mr. Besser and Curly Joe Derita get the fullest recognition as actual members of The Three Stooges. They truly deserve to be reevaluated and honored for their years of service as a member of that famous comedy team. They took their own style of comic personalities and incorporated those manners into the fold of the group. They added a fresh and totally new look as well as preparing the Stooges for a new generation of loyal fans. They both never tried to imitate Curly or Shemp. They paved their own road.

Joe Besser served the shortest stint as and a member of the Stooges. Two years to be exact. Curly Joe Derita twelve years. Both men had a long lists of solo careers before and after their association as The Three Stooges. They were professional comedians who through long years of work developed their unique own individualism as funny clowns. Columbia the studio they had both been employed at before being recruited to join the Stooges had them each headlining their own short film series. Joe Besser did ten two reelers and Joe Derita (as he was then billed) did four. For more about their own starring series, please refer to my book, ONLY ONE STOOGE.

What I have done with this book is taken apart both men and their individual work as a stooge. I have chronologically analyzed the last sixteen two reelers and the last starring seven feature films (including KOOK'S TOUR). In my first edition which is still available on Kindle, I had really only scratched the surface of each film. In this revised edition I will further take apart each short and feature film and further analyze as well as add more to this project. I will also be adding more pictures to help illustrate what I am trying very hard to convey in my appreciation of these two men.

It is also of high importance that we also examine briefly the careers of The Three Stooges as a whole. This will help to understand and better appreciate the two JOES who came into the fold. I really do hope you find this revised edition a major plus in helping to build up the reputation of two individuals who gave The Three Stooges a fresh and different look than the years before they became actual members of the most beloved comedy team the world has known. Their contributions kept the flame burning and forever helped keep The Three Stooges in the memories of their most loyal fans (Me included).

ANALYZING THE COLUMBIA SHORTS DEPARTMENT:

INCARNATION	YEARS	SHORTS	FILMS
Ted Healy and His Stooges (Moe, Larry and Shemp)	1930-34	6	8
Moe, Larry and Curly	1934-47	97	11
Moe, Larry and Shemp ▶	1947-56	77	3
◀ Moe, Larry and Joe	1957-58	16	1
Moe, Larry and Curly Joe ▶	1959-70	2	8

Columbia was founded by Harry Cohn in 1924. In the earliest beginnings the studio had a rather difficult time in establishing its importance in the film industry. But it wouldn't be long before the studio would start to make a serious name for itself. In 1933 Cohn formed the shorts department. For the next twenty five years this department would help the studio overcome some of its financial struggles. While the studio distributed its major feature films, the shorts department became a strength for theaters to recon with. Cohn used the popularity of these two reelers as leverage over his established major movie making. With the high demand for these two reelers, Cohn used his lower budget pictures to be tagged along with these short films. Theater owners were forced to show pictures that were not the type of grade A features that the movie going public really wanted to see.

Harry Cohn hired Jules White to organize the shorts department. Jules White was an accomplished comedy writer and director. Jules in order to direct some of these films had Hugh McCollum a business manager for the shorts department start sharing some of the production chores. Both men divided the units into two separate entities. An average of twenty five shorts a year were released from 1934 and on.

A staff of competent writers were added as well as sound effects technicians, editors and a long string of supporting players who helped the several individual series prosper. The Three Stooges were added to the roster in 1934. As the years progressed the stooges and their films became the top money makers for the shorts department. Out of all the individual series created they lasted the longest. The stooges were the only shorts produced by the late 1950s.

In their heyday The Three Stooges developed into an excellent comedy team. Their films were in more demand by the public than any other series created by the studio. With top writers, directors and the huge line of excellent supporting players who the stooges played off of, the chemistry within these shorts spread out like a wild fire! But another important thing was that The Three Stooges could carry a film all by themselves! They grew into their established characters and really didn't need a director to direct them but act more as a traffic cop directing the other players in the background. They knew how to get laughs. They pretty much directed themselves. Their humor was instilled within each of them.

Moe Howard was the team's leader on and off the screen. His character in these films was the guy who bossed and slapped around his two cohorts. Larry Fine could side with Moe or Curly. It depended on what he felt might better suit him. He was the perfect foil for both of his partners. He could be just as idiotic as Curly or just as aggressive as Moe. Curly was the most naive out of the three. A small child stuck in the body of a fat, bald headed grown man. The perfect sap! His mannerisms often came in conflict with his two frustrated partners. Together these three simpletons helped to create the magic of golden comedy in the short films they starred in as a perfect assembled comedy trio.

From 1934 up until the 1940s the stooges were widely recognized. They grew within these years and helped to produce some hilarious comedy classics. But by the mid-1940s Curly's personal physical and mental health was deteriorating. On top of all that the studio's budget restraints were being slashed. Overall quality was being sacrificed to meet much smaller financial budgets. Theaters were double Billing feature films in exchange for the shorts which were having a hard time getting a market. Many major motion picture studios had already closed their own personal shorts departments. They were all now concentrating of big budget features. Laurel and Hardy had stopped making short films in 1935. The popular Our Gang series had been sold to MGM in 1938 and their high qualities of short films took an immediate swing for the worse. By 1944 they were no longer being made. Columbia would eventually downsize their two reelers to just two series than just one.

In order to keep within the budgets the studio began using old stock footage from previous shorts and worked new footage around the old. This became the norm in making their making the two reelers. With Curly not being able to do his physical and verbal tricks and Moe and Larry now taking more of the slapstick comedy onto themselves the use of older films inserted into the newer ones helped to maintain the overall freshness of the comedy presented. These films ranged from being fair to bad. Larry and Moe needed a third stooge to play off of and with Curly being ill it just seemed to lose the old magic spark from years before. Curly had lost weight, his facial features became withdrawn and the delivery of his lines became wooden and squeaky. He was not the Curly audiences had come to know and love!

In 1945 while working on the film, HALFWITS HOLIDAY, Curly suffered a debilitating stroke that closed his career with the stooges forever. It was a sad lost. In 1946 Moe's older brother Shemp rejoined the team. He quickly helped to restore the stooges waning popularity. The comedies rose from their weaknesses and blossomed into a whole new batch of fresh and funny comedies. The Three Stooges under a new middle stooge for the next several years reinvented themselves and created a string of new classic comedies. It was a breath of pure fresh air despite the loss of Curly. Shemp didn't imitate his younger brother he forged an independent road for himself and together with Moe and Larry a brand new Three Stooges was born!

With Shemp now in the fold, using old Curly stock footage just wouldn't match up with the new films being created. The Three Stooges were back into creating brand new, fresh and funny two reelers. The transition had very little difficulties. The primary reason for this was that Shemp had in fact been the original middle stooge when the trio had originally worked with Ted Healey. Curly replaced Shemp in 1932 and now Shemp after 13 years later was replacing Curly.

A good majority of the films with Shemp were called box comedies because most of the two reelers produced were indoors in a specific setting of different rooms or just one room. Outside shots were mainly used as a part of a narrative and rarely did the stooges in this period perform outdoors. This greatly reduced the costs of making these new shorts. Sets from major motion pictures were borrowed to create new and inventive ideas. Despite the financial burdens this helped to elevate the shorts in their personal qualities. The writers used the many interior props to help move the stories from one scene to the next. The editing in these particular shorts thrived because the tighter they were the better the short. Another factor within these films was that the stories became more coherent. Unlike the cartoonist action from the Curly films, this new batch of stooges shorts offered an identifiable plot structure and the gags flowed in ease with the story being told. Curly obviously fit appropriately in the context of films that over exaggerated their individual stories, but Shemp was better suited in more situation comedies than films with loose attachments. Not to say that the comedy in these new films weren't exaggerated, they were but the gags and jokes weren't thrown in just to get a simple laugh they actually helped in moving the story forward.

Curly fitted well in the loose connected shorts of years earlier. His agility, girth and verbal trickery were what projected the shorts forward. Moe and Larry were natural in their reactions to Curly's mannerisms. Those films were radically different from the new films being produced during the Shemp era. This new transition had to be different, because Shemp was better suited to these type of sitcom comedies. Moe and Larry adapted to this new format and quite honestly their more refined humor added a certain charisma. All three blended well with one another.

Now also in this period the writers experimented with the stooges. In so doing they separated the team within their films. Also they tried in two shorts three dimensional formats that were unique to say the least. The inventive scare comedies that came out during this time were very well constructed and the ghosts and monsters seemed quite authentic. In these the boy's scared reactions as well as the villains playing their roles semi straight to the stooges comical slapstick and verbal puns helped to make these particular shorts move at a frantic and hilarious pace. The atmosphere in these scare comedies were quite realistic in delivering their own style of pure fright as well as comic delight.

Unfortunately as the years entered into the mid-1950s the quality sank to a new low. Once again old films were inserted into the new ones and the original stories from earlier Shemp films were refurbished to make them appear as completed new shorts. It was very rare at this time for something original to be made. And if it was an original comedy more than likely the refurbished films looked way better and usually moved at a faster pace. The budgets for these films were quickly beginning to show their cheapness.

After Shemp had passed away in November of 1955 a double was used as a stand in for him in the last four films produced under the Shemp titles. Moe and Larry were the sole focus of delivering the bulk of the new comedy in the new filmed scenes inserted around the old footage. Stunt double, actor Joe Palma filled in as Shemp's stand in and was seen only from the back, under masks and having his full face covered by hand held props. Shemp dominated the old stock footage.

Now this type of film making couldn't go on forever so the studio began looking for another middle stooge. Joe Besser was recruited into the team and for the next two years the void was temporarily filled. Despite the new breath of fresh air the films took an unsuspected nose dive. Columbia had lost interest in making quality shorts. They had a contract to fulfill and they rushed this new series of stooges in order to complete an obligation. It was very heartbreaking to see a commodity that helped the studio earn their fortune turned into a unit that the upper heads felt that they now had no real need to care about! It was a sad time for The Three Stooges.

After Besser had left the act, Curly Joe Derita came in as the final middle stooge. The shorts department had closed shop in 1958 and now with the resurgence of new popularity, The Three Stooges were headlining their own starring feature film series. Columbia had decided earlier to release the old Three Stooges shorts to the new medium at the time television. A generation of new Stooges fans were born. By the time the mid-1960s had arrived The Three Stooges were now the most sought after comedy team in show business.

ANALYZING JOE:

The Three Stooges began as a vaudeville act in the early 1920s. Their mentor and leader Ted Healey headlined the act and the stooges (Not billed as stooges.) were more or less sidekicks. The group first consisted of Moe Howard and his older brother Shemp Howard (Larry Fine would join the act a few years later.) Healey was the straight man to the chaotic and often hilarious Moe and Shemp. By the time they made their first motion picture deal with Twentieth Century the act included Healey and four stooges, Moe, Larry, Shemp and Fred Sanborn. The film was SOUP TO NUTS (1930). Healey had not come off as well as he had personally hoped, but Moe, Larry and Shemp had made an incredible impression in the few short scenes they dominated. It was a small prelude of what was to come.

By 1932, Shemp had left the act for greener pastures. His replacement was his and Moe's younger brother Jerome Howard. Adopting the name Curly because of his mirth, weight and bald head, this new set of Three Stooges with Healey still in control took an almost immediate upswing in popularity. But it wasn't until the two Howard brothers and Fine broke away from their original straight man that The Three Stooges came into their own.

Now working in the shorts department for Columbia studios Curly, Larry and Moe for the next twelve years had movie audiences howling with laughter. Their personal brand of slapstick, verbal jokes and the incredible chemistry that the three shared, along with top comedy writers and directors created a vibrant library of short funny films. The Three Stooges were at the height of super success.

Sadly in 1945 Curly suffered a debilitating stroke that forced him out of the group. Shemp came back and for the next ten years, although he wasn't Curly, created another batch of hilarious two reel comedies. Shemp had in fact lifted the team out from a bad year of mediocrity films (Curly had suffered minor strokes that effected his performances for the last couple of years before leaving the team. Moe and Larry pretty much carried the bulk of the comedy in these last dozen of films.) Shemp didn't imitate his younger brother, instead he brought his own salty humor and integrated it into the act and this new and fresh approach to the team gave the comedy a more three dimensional look.

In November of 1955 Shemp Howard suffered a massive, fatal heart attack. Once again Moe and Larry were left without a third stooge. Still having to fill their obligation under studio contract they desperately needed a new third stooge. This is where Joe Besser was hired on to be the new third stooge. From 1956 up until 1959, Besser was now an official member of the trio. By this time the Columbia studio shorts had become weak and cheaply made. Old film stock footage from earlier Stooges comedies were stitched to newer films and used to recreate somewhat shoddy and poorly edited two reelers marked as new and fresh comedies. The shorts department was dying and Joe Besser happened to step into a period that produced the last sixteen two reelers that got stamped with being the worse films ever created during this time.

A lot of people will dismiss Joe as an actual member of the Stooges. But in all truth the blame shouldn't be directed at this one individual. Joe Besser was indeed a serious member of The Three Stooges. There is a lot one has to fully be aware of when one goes to analyze the bulk of these last Stooges comedies. And let's not forget that despite the majority of these 16 two reelers being cheaply produced, a handful of them were quite interesting and delivered some genuine humor. Even the very weak films had isolated moments of hysterical comedy. Also in this period new ideas were introduced and although many didn't work, there were some of those new jokes that carried over into the Curly Joe era. Let's examine the last Stooges films and the reasons behind their individual failings, then let's review each and every one of those films and rediscover the pure delight that as kids growing up we just couldn't wait for a Besser film to appear on our television screens. We all loved Curly, we all admired Shemp, but there was something about Joe that kept us wanting to see more.

TED HEALEY ERA (1925-1934):

Now although Healey and the two Howard brothers, Moe and Shemp had already been an established act since

1922, the real beginning in my personal opinion was when Larry Fine joined the team. Here is where the real chemistry took shape and began evolving into the future act we all know and love so well.

From 1925 up until they made their first motion picture Healey and his Stooges tested their material in front of a live audience. They quickly learned what got laughs and what didn't. They were able to create routines and further strengthen their individual personalities to form a well-balanced team. By the time they made their debut in the film SOUP TO NUTS, they were an established team. Movie going audiences that had never seen our heroes got a glimpse of the things to come! But also in this very beginning, the transformations, Shemp departed and in his place came Curly.

A half dozen two reelers, another handful of feature film appearances The Three Stooges were slowly realizing that Healey wasn't a necessity they needed. They could move forward without him. They could be funnier just as an assembled trio than just as second bananas to an over inflated ego demonstrated by Healey who not only bullied them on screen but off as well.

But the years of working with Ted proved to be a very valuable experience. In all honesty had they not been a part of Healey's assembled act, they could have possibly never formed their success as The Three Stooges! Their personal triumphs and failures during this period made

24

them into the famous comedy team that carried their careers for over forty years.

CURLY, LARRY AND MOE (1934-1946):

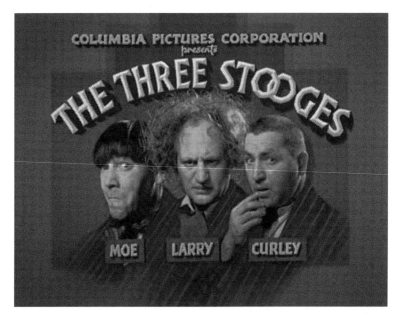

They were all young, ambitious, and willing to do almost whatever it took to make a success out of their leaving Ted Healey! Moe Howard took over the bossy Healey role. Larry Fine became the guy in the middle who blew in the direction of whichever way the wind was blowing. Curly was the over grown child, naive, unaware of his personal surroundings and the other two's fall guy. Together all three developed a deeper and more refined act. They enhanced whatever film they played in. It was a new adventure that needed nourishment. 100% of their efforts went into the making of their specialized comedy. With each and every succeeded two reel The Three Stooges captured the publics' full attention! And as the years progressed they just seemed to get better and funnier than before. They reintroduced the slapstick comedy that rooted from the age of silent films.

When one watches a film with Curly one has the impression that they are watching twenty minutes of a live action cartoon. The comedy is chaotic and deliberately fast paced. Moe the boss is just as dopey as the two who follow him, but he is also the most ignorant of his less than perfect personality. Larry can be Moe's sidekick or Curly's bumbling partner that more than likely guarantees that Moe is going to get mad and slap him silly. Curly is the dumbest of the three and he obviously hasn't a clue as to the stupid things he does that projects all problems to his two cohorts. Together they screw up whatever they are assigned to do.

The off the wall sound effects add to the charm of each film. When Moe bops Curly on the head we laugh instead of cringing. Their individual facial expressions add to the humor presented. They are three over grown children unaccustomed to the imperfections that populate their world! They snub high society, they frustrate authority, henpecked husbands, overly fresh with beautiful women, inadvertently thwart the bad guys, are easily scared silly by ghosts and monsters, they champion the oppressed and make a simple chore into a total, nonsense, huge mess. They are the essential Three Stooges. Larry, Moe and Curly are the ones who set the standards of the humor derived from their comedy two reelers. We measure all the rest that come later to these three imperfect clowns. We fail to recognize the individual talents and the unique differences that the much later middle stooges have to offer.

Okay these three set the record. But we tend to forget that Curly followed Shemp! That Shemp had the unpleasant task of replacing a younger brother who was ill. Curly's later years as a stooge when he was deteriorating from a series of small strokes made it impossible for the act to continue as they had before. Moe had to direct his anger more toward Larry. Larry suddenly became the middle stooge. Curly became Larry. The act had lost its momentum and the electric spark was slowly diminishing. Both Moe and Larry had to keep the act strong and the films writers and directors had to divert the bulk of the comedy to two instead of three. Curly's physical appearance looked haggard and he seemed thinner than his two partners. His voice had changed and he could no longer project the high pitched vocal tricks. This is where old stock footage was borrowed from previous films to help complete a new film that might go into over production because Curly's health created sudden changes on how a particular film might be made. On rare occasions the old Curly sparked, but for the most part the weaker

Curly dominated on how a film was produced and this was a very distressing time for all involved.

SHEMP, LARRY AND MOE (1946-1956):

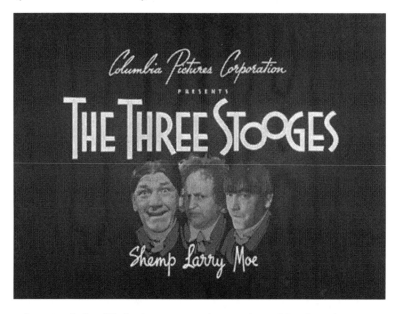

After Curly had left the team, Shemp his older brother stepped in to take his place as third stooge. For the next ten years The Three Stooges received a second lease on their careers as clowns. Shemp presented a different personality that actually blended perfectly with the already established personalities of Moe and Larry. The stories moved away from the cartoonist films of Curly and presented a more coherent environment that audiences could readily identify with. The films seemed more properly constructed. The looseness that had been prevalent with Curly and worked very well with him did not fit in the formula created by this new set of Stooges. This new approach added a much needed fresh look and feel. The Shemp films placed our stooges in more realistic situations. The bad guys were darker and sinister. The monsters and ghosts more frightening. The comedy derived from the stooges over reacting. The one liners moved the story along and weren't there just to get a simple laugh.

Larry seemed to grow as a more emphasized partner. Suddenly The Three Stooges seemed more as a team than what they had been before. It was all together something very similar and yet very different. And yet it worked! This new set of stooges moved into a realm that would have been foreign to the Curly films. Shemp was more aggressive towards Moe and Larry. Larry and Shemp were better equipped when it came to defending themselves from the constant tempers that came out from Moe. They were whole.

The scare comedies were brilliantly paced. The scare reaction from each Stooge seemed genuinely unique and quite funny. Shemp paved his own way and his unique salty humor perfectly meshed with his two partners. The first five years gave us some sharp pointed humor and a very healthy variety of classic comedies. There were some awful clunkers in that mix bag of shorts, but for the most part the majority entertained.

By the mid-fifties most of the Shemp films became remakes of earlier films with a heavy load of old stock footage. Sometimes the old footage dominated the few new scenes inserted. The later Shemp two reelers became tiresome and the editing could be very sloppy. The new isolated gags reworked into an old story didn't seem to ignite the freshness compared to the older clips and the films looked disjointed and it seemed that the shorts department really didn't care about the quality of the films they distributed. Unfortunately when Shemp died that was where Joe Besser stepped into the act. The studio made very little effort to sharpen their continued output of comedy two reelers. As each film progressed the overall quality in editing, sets, acting and humor suffered tremendously. Joe Besser was caught between a rock and a hard place! Within two short years Moe had lost two brothers. Larry was also feeling this loss. The Three Stooges had to once again (And this wouldn't be the last time!) face a new unforeseen beginning. They had to take stock of themselves and work past the obvious obstacles that invaded their last 16 two reel comedies.

LARRY, MOE AND JOE BESSER (1957-1959):

The shortest stint as an actual member of The Three Stooges, Joe Besser had the sad task of following Shemp. On top of all that the Columbia shorts department was slowly dying. The studio didn't care anymore about the product it put out. Also in the very beginning Besser had stipulated in his contract that any major rough housing be diverted from him (although that would eventually change). So now it became a rather strenuous position for Larry who had most of Moe's hot temper directed onto him. Another factor was that both Moe and Larry seemed tired and played out. Twenty four years of doing slapstick comedy had worn them both down. It was a very difficult period for The Three Stooges.

Just as Besser, Fine and Howard had begun to warm up to one another the shorts department closed and Joe sadly had to leave the act. In these last few years the stooges had to learn how to overcome so many difficult obstacles. Eventually they found themselves and in between all the bad, they managed to in a handful of shorts come out shining and those isolated gems although far from being classic comedies rose above the usual weak norm. Even in the weaker films there were some rare, but hilarious moments that came shining through. And towards the end Joe began taking more of Moe's personal punishing. Unfortunately at this time this particular group of stooges was fast coming to an abrupt ending.

To say that Joe was the reason behind the poor output of shorts at this particular awkward time is a serious misconception! He gave 100% in delivering his part of the comedy. He was a funny little fat man who tried to breathe some fresh air into this new trio of stooges. He was caught being compared to his predecessors and that in itself was totally unfair. His own child mannerisms were in fact all his own. He didn't try to imitate Curly or Shemp. He brought his own unique style of comedy to this group. But walking in the footsteps of two popular shadows put him at a disadvantage. Also the fact that he was handed the chore of remaking classic comedies already done by Curly and Shemp. His own individualism was crushed. The small amount of originality in these last 16 films didn't give him the room to grow on his own accords. Also if the truth was to be known, both Moe and Larry were at many times just going through the paces. Much of their comedy lacked spark and ingenuity. The deaths of Curly and Shemp had too weigh heavy on both of their hearts. Another new beginning with an uncertain future had to seem quite burdensome. Finding out what worked and what didn't work for this new set of stooges was an impossible task. They couldn't test their new act in front of a live audience so that left them not really knowing on how well or poorly they were doing.

Another important factor to consider was age. All three men were in their mid to late fifties. So there were many gags that fell flat because watching old men perform scenes that are more acceptable at a younger age than at the age they were in. Not to say that all the physical high jinx was in appropriate, it's just that some of the comedy looked rather distasteful instead of being funny. And matching old stock footage from ten to twenty years ago looked pale compared to the new filmed scenes. There were a few shorts where the new scenes looked old compared to the actual older footage.

Out of the 16 final short films that the stooges completed during this period, only six stand out as really being above the usual average. While the remaining ten ranged from mildly interesting to downright disasters. But to say that those bad shorts had no merit what so ever would not be quite so true. Their original concepts had some potential even if they were remakes of other past films. The editing, dead spaces, lack of energy throughout, as well as some rather stilted directing added to these films being stale in comparisons to their counterparts. If they had tried to follow what the six above average films had presented its just possible that the entire bulk of these 16 two reelers might have given The Three Stooges in their final years of doing these films a much higher appreciation with movie going audiences.

Although these films were far from being classics, MUSCLE UP A LITTLE CLOSER, A MERRY MIX UP, SPACE SHIP SAPPY, FLYING SAUCER DAFFY, OUTER SPACE JITTERS, and OILS

WELL THAT ENDS WELL, gave the stooges a rare chance to actually shine within these six shorts.

While films like, PIES AND GUYS, SAPPY BULLFIGHTERS, RUSTY ROMEOS, FIFI BLOWS HER TOP, HOOFS AND GOOFS and HORSING AROUND, although most of these remakes of other films were average comedies that presented mild entertainment.

However films like, QUIZ WHIZ, GUNS A POPPIN, SWEET AND HOT and TRIPLE CROSSED, should have never been made! These films did nothing to enhance the trio's Careers. In fact these films were a huge total embarrassment. Joe Besser had he been judged solely on these four shorts most definitely would have vanished from stooge history.

The biggest irony of all was television in the 1950s. It sealed the coffin on the stooge's short films. However it also was responsible for reviving their popularity years later when Columbia sold their films to that particular medium of entertainment. People now could sit in the comforts of their homes and watch the brand new comedy sitcoms. Theaters were busy presenting double features so the market for two reelers had been limited and the studios had a hard time making profits. So budgets were slashed and the remaining stooge comedies suffered tremendously. It was a terrible time for everyone involved in creating short film comedies. By the time Besser joined the stooges, they were the last series of shorts produced.

The Three Stooges held the longest record of working in a short film department.

In the pages following I am going to break down each of the last 16 two reelers that the stooges made. I am going to point out their flaws as well as their merits. I am going to do my own summaries as well as my own personal reviews so although you might not totally agree on all of my personal opinions I hope you'll at least agree that this project I've set forth is one that is long overdue. Maybe the people who disregard Joe Besser as an actual member of the stooges will look at him a bit differently. Maybe through this Joe Besser, Larry Fine and Moe Howard in this particular period of Three Stooges comedies produced will gain a higher level of personal respect and a higher level of overall appreciation.

THE SUPPORTING ACTORS:

I cannot go forward without acknowledging the actors who supported the Three Stooges from this period under the Joe Besser titles. They helped to try and lift the poor quality of these films from the average norm of poor. They deserve being mentioned as well as applauded along with the stooges for giving these last 16 two reelers a strong breath of life and delivering their own individual style of humor. It wasn't an easy task but they all prevailed and despite the majority of these films just being fair and the handful that was heavily below the average of poor, there were moments that came shining through! Now let's not forget the half dozen of shorts that rose above the norm and succeeded in being clever and ingenious in presenting the old spark of what The Three Stooges used to have and the supporting players in these particular shorts delivered a slam bang form of pure undiluted entertainment! They are as follows:

Emil Sitka, Harriette Tarler, Frank Sully, Joe Palma, Vernon Dent, Benny Rubin, Doreen Woodbury, Marilyn Hanold, Lorraine Crawford, Nanette Bordeaux, Suzanne Ridgeway, Diana Darrin, Jeanne Carmen, Maxine Gates, Ruth Godfrey, Matt Murphy, Connie Cezan, Gene Roth, Philip Van Zandt, Dan Blocker, Arline Hunter, Greta Thyssen, Milton Frome, Bill Brauer, Vanda Dupre, Christine

McIntyre, Yvette Reynard, Al Thompson, Charles Conklin, Wanda D'Ottoni, Helen Dickson, Symona Boniface, Barbara Slater, Muriel Landers, Gail Bonney, Bek Nelson, Angela Stevens, Mary Ainslee, Johnny Kascier, George

Lewis, Eddie Laughton, Cy Schindell.

41

HOOFS AND GOOFS

January 31, 1957

15minutes

Directed By: Jules White

With: Benny Rubin, Harriette Tarler and Tony, the Wonder Horse.

Larry, Moe and Joe are mourning over the loss of their beloved Sister Birdie. However it's Joe who is taking it the hardest out of the three men. Moe in order to snap Joe out of his depressing state plays on Joe believing in reincarnation. Later while walking on the streets, The Three Stooges come across a horse who is discovered to be their lost sister reincarnated. They bring their sister up into their top floor apartment. The landlord who lives with his daughter on the floor below is suspicious of the Stooges' weird behavior. On investigating he is terribly tormented while the Stooges scramble around to hide the horse. After he is literally thrown out of their apartment, the Stooges discover that Bertie is with child and they all go about in a slapstick melee to help deliver the new colt. After the pony is born, Joe wakes up from dreaming and his sister is still very much alive and well. When he relates his dream to her, she dumps a huge bowl of potato salad over his head.

This was the first film to feature Joe Besser as the new middle stooge. The premise is clever, but the film as a whole is slightly below average. Most of the humor in this film comes from the supporting player Benny Rubin. Larry and Moe seem a bit out of place playing second fiddle to a horse. Joe, however makes a rather unclear debut. His character seems over dominant almost as if he's the boss of the team. There are some very funny sequences but most of the comedy comes from Mr. Rubin who plays the stooges' landlord.

43

Harriette Tarler's role is just incidental as Rubin's daughter who reacts to her father's comic mishaps. The special effects and editing are top notch and the physical action between the stooges is heavily placed on Moe and Larry. At the time of Besser's induction into the group he had it stipulated in his contract that there would be no rough slapstick placed on his immediate body. In order to redirect the violence away from Joe the writers gave most of the violent physical comedy to Benny Rubin. It is Rubin who is hit by falling plaster from the ceiling below the stooges' apartment. Birdie the horse kicks him face first into some fly paper, he falls down the stairs, (off screen sound effects) and he unknowingly drinks milk with ether and passes out.

Moe and Larry share a funny scene where Moe trips over a chair left in the middle of the kitchen floor while he is holding a basin filled with water and when he goes and refills the basin it is Larry who knocks him over with the swinging door. Joe Besser has some isolated funny scenes. One where he bonks Moe on the head and has his balled fist bounce back and hit him in his own head. Trying to open the bottle of ether and knocking himself out.

If you're looking for laugh out loud comedy this film has very little to offer in that category. But the film does move at a steady pace and instead of delivering high volume laughs it settles with raising simple, pleasant smiles. It may not be the stooges standard of regular comedy but it really isn't a bad film.

The verbal exchanges between all the players are interesting and help to move the story along. The final ending of having Joe wake up and discover that all that had proceeded was in fact just a dream dissolves quite nicely. The dream has a conclusion and the final gag of Moe (in drag) breaking a casserole bowl over Joe's head with creamy potato salad in it is a fitting slapstick finale.

Joe Besser's debut is a mild transition into the stooges. The writers had to work around the stipulations that Joe had inserted into his contract. They do a fine job of diverting the heavy violence away from Joe but in doing this they focus on a supporting player to deliver the bulk of the humor and this robs the stooges of being themselves. The Three Stooges come off as second bananas in a two reeler that they were supposed to be the major stars of. That's why this film is below par. It's not that the film is bad it just isn't a full fledge stooges comedy.

A few films later a sequel of sorts was made that actually incorporated all of the Three Stooges into the entire frame work of the film. Unfortunately the comedy in that film was mild too. The next stooges' film to follow this first one was a definite major improvement! It should have been the initial film to introduce Joe.

MUSCLE UP A LITTLE CLOSER

February28, 1957

16minutes

Directed By: Jules White

With: Maxine Gates, Harriette Tarler, Ruth Godfrey and Matt Murphy.

Larry, Moe and Joe are calling on their girlfriends. While visiting Joe's fiancé discovers that her engagement ring has been stolen. The Stooges suspect their Foreman from the warehouse that they and the girls work at. Playing private eyes, The Three Stooges search the warehouse and find the ring in their boss's locker. They confront him and a hilarious wrestling match ensues until Joe's girlfriend, Tiny intercedes and beats the boss to a pulp.

This film was a way, high, up above average short! This should have been the short to introduce Joe Besser as the new stooge! Unlike its predecessor this is pure Three Stooges. It may not rate as a comedy classic but it comes close to anything holding that distinguished honor. It is undoubtedly the best stooges' film to come out at this particular period of time. It moves at a fast pace and delivers the serious laughter that had been solely missed in the first release. Like the first film its plot is simple. Unlike the first film the stooges are a stronger unity. They play off of one another brilliantly. The supporting players get laughs but don't over shadow the boys.

48

The physical slapstick is in perfect timing. Joe is worked into the fold and although he doesn't participate in the last battle with the villain he still comes out incredibly hilarious. The scene where Joe believes he's having a heart attack is pure hysterical comedy. When Moe pretends to be a qualified doctor and gives Joe a drink of water and ask him to say "pink pills" and Joe sprays his mouthful of water on both Moe and Larry the gag is so stupid it's funny. The entire premise is exaggerated and the comedy takes top priority. It's not a complicated film and the editing is almost flawless.

The final wrestling scene with Moe and Larry taking on Matt Murphy is a pure delight. When Joe's girlfriend Tiny (who is anything but tiny) takes on Mr. Murphy after he has beaten up both Moe and Larry is a very fast and funny physical fight. Her heavy weight plopping on the villain would be a wrestling fans delight. This is what The Three Stooges were all about.

If only the rest of the shorts to follow would have been as clever and funny as this one! Not to say that the next film or the films after that were all bad, but this one recreated what The Three Stooges had once been. Not implying or comparing Joe to Curly or Shemp but comparing the quality, comedy, editing, timing and a simple plot device that concentrates purely on gags to move the story forward. The film works and that in itself is a major step upward.

49

Muscle Up A Little Closer, also introduced both Moe and Larry without their trademark hairstyles. Both men under the suggestion of Joe Besser combed their hair backs and five more films would follow suit. It was an interesting idea to do something fresh and different. At first it probably caught movie audiences off guard but the fast, deliberate pace of this short quickly dissolved any wonder if this was in actuality a full fledge Three Stooges two reeler.

The Three Stooges in their solo scenes packing boxes and making a mess of things has several highlights. This includes the above mentioned, "Pink Pills" routine that was the funniest piece of material produced during all the years that Joe was a Stooge. Another good gag follows Joe as he accidentally drops a crate of fresh eggs and uses a blow torch to make scrambled eggs and then proceeds to shovel the cooked eggs back into the box. During this escapade, Joe gets retaliation by Moe who uses the torch to set fire to Joe's behind.

A MERRY MIX UP

March28, 1957

15minutes

Directed By: Jules White

With: Frank Sully, Nanette Bordeaux, Suzanne Ridgeway, Hariette Tarler, Diana Darrin, Ruth Godfrey White and Jeanne Carmen.

The Three Stooges play a set of identical triplets who anger girlfriends, wives and a frustrated waiter.

A few notches below the previous film, A MERRY MIX UP presents a unique premise. The Three Stooges play a set of identical triplets. The gags are funny but the film as a whole suffers from a lot of dead spots splattered within the framework. And the cheap settings are a flaw but the short doesn't restrain its humor. Despite its obvious flaws the short does move at a fast pace and this seems to over shadow the cheap production. The editing is clumsy and a little bit disjointed. What truly makes this short work is the comedy of reactions from the stooges and supporting players. Frank Sully as the frustrated waiter is a perfect foil for the boys. The chase scene could have been a bit longer but it serves its purpose in bringing the finale to a fitting closing end.

The humor exchanged through the stooges with one another is fresh and inventive. They along with the supporting players rise above the above mentioned flaws. Also this is one short where the flaws are forced into the content of the comedy. It actually enhances a certain charm. It might not be a totally original concept but the exaggerated idea of doing a twin comedy with triplets is pure genius! One could only wish that this had been made in the format of a feature film. So many inspirational ideas could have been developed. However when one thinks about this short it immediately says Joe Besser! He has the bulk of running gags and verbal jokes that help build this two reeler into an above average comedy.

Larry Fine has his personal shining moments as well! His delivery of one liners, his physical slapstick is perfectly timed. Moe whose aggressiveness is toned down plays well off of his two partners and despite his frustration with them his physical and verbal punishment fits well into the way plot moves.

I remember as a kid growing up in the early seventies that this particular short subject was among my personal favorites. After school when it was time for the stooges to appear on television I always hoped and sometimes prayed that one of the two shorts being broadcasted would be this particular film. It was just something about its ideas that inspired my own personal imaginations. To me as a kid this was The Three Stooges at their kiddie best!

Here for the first time The Three Stooges aimed their comedy at a younger audience. It wouldn't be long before Columbia would sell the first seventy films of the stooges to television in the late 1950s. They would sky rocket to new heights of popularity. It wasn't just a phase neither! For the next thirty to forty years the stooges would rise as the kings of comedy. Their constant showing of films on television and revivals in theaters projected their super surge of power over a generation that had never seen the stooges in their heydays! And when you really think about this Joe Besser came at a time when the stooges were aiming to entertain youngsters. His brand of humor complimented this new transformation. Whether it was a foretelling of what was to come or just pure perfect timing the stooges in this period didn't particularly aim their comedy at adults. I personally believed that Larry, Moe and Joe began to set the new norm. I believe they unknowingly set the stage for Curly Joe Derita who would a couple of years later replace Joe Besser. So maybe we should open our minds a little more and try to forget our adult world when watching a Besser short and totally look at these last films with the old child in all of us.

SPACE SHIP SAPPY

April18, 1957

16minutes

Directed By: Jules White

With: Benny Rubin, Harriette Tarler, Doreen Woodbury, Marilyn Hanold, Lorraine Crawford and Emil Sitka.

Joe, Larry and Moe are unemployed sailors living as vagrants. One day they find a job in the want ads. They meet up with an eccentric professor and his daughter and soon embark on a trip into outer space. They land on the planet Venus where they encounter three vampires and a giant monster lizard. After escaping from these horrors they inadvertently knock out the professor and his daughter. After launching the rocket back into space, the boys wreck the controls and plummet down surely to crash! The scene dissolves and The Three Stooges are at a convention receiving an award for being the biggest liars in the world.

Another A+ film! For the first time the stooges are taken out of the real world and propelled into outer space. This film travels back into the era of live action cartoons. Maybe not as high as the films made with Curly but not so far removed from the shorts produced in the 1930s. The stooges are bums searching for work and what they find for employment is far beyond this world.

The individual sight gags, special effects and the physical comedy all mesh nicely together. Benny Rubin doesn't over shadow the stooges as he had done in HOOFS AND GOOFS! He is funny but he steps aside in order for the boys to deliver their humor. The tickling scene goes on just a few seconds longer than one might want but that seems to be the only minor flaw in this short.

The Three Stooges show an incredible spark of energy and they interact with one another very well. Hariette Tarler as the first leading lady in the new stooges' period delivers an excellent nonchalant attitude towards the boys. She and Rubin once again play the role of father and daughter. This chemistry seems genuine. They work incredibly well as being foils for the stooges.

The scene where the stooges are to get injected with shots before they embark on their trip is undoubtedly another one of the funniest set pieces ever introduced in a stooge's comedy. Their individual frights seem very authentic. Once again some evident cheapness does appear but because of the deliberate humor it is easy to overlook this little setback. The wild imagination that this short presents compliments the antics of The Three Stooges.

From a below average introduction with HOOFS AND GOOFS the next three films that followed it proved that Joe Besser could work as a member of The Three Stooges. If only they had continued to be consistent with the quality of shorts that followed this film. If that had been the case it's just possible that the Besser films would have gained a higher respect from stooge fans. It's ashamed that the next short almost deliberately set the boys back. Instead of building on this high succession of funny films the next one nearly crippled the high expected results that these previous three films began to set as a standard in the new trio of stooges. Now the films had sporadic moments of isolated gags stuffed into bad films. The better projects were sadly sandwiched in between the average and bad! This created a rather disjointed relationship with the stooges and their loving public. This was where the comparisons of Joe, Shemp and Curly probably began to take root. Sadly this proved to be the lot in the finale string of short films and poor Besser was overshadowed by these poor shorts that seemed to be a plague spreading.

What's incredible is that even if the short was beyond the lowest of low budgets, if the material, direction and story inspired, The Three Stooges could make magic. They were able to shift an audiences' attention for the most part away from the cheapness that went into making these final two reelers. Unfortunately that wasn't the case with the next short released after this one.

GUNS A POPPIN

June13, 1957

16minutes

Directed By: Jules White

With: Vernon Dent, Frank Sully and Joe Palma.

Moe is on trial for assaulting both Larry and Joe with an axe. In flashback we see that Moe is a very sick man who is also in terrible debt. Larry and Joe decide to take Moe out into the country for some fresh air, peace and quiet. But it is anything but tranquility. First they have a run in with a black bear and then are in the middle of a gunfight with a sheriff chasing a wanted bad guy. Once the story is revealed, the judge immediately dismisses the charges against Moe.

The first Besser film to be a refurbishing of an old Curly film. Unfortunately it is also the first real weak film of this period. The gags and physical comedy look forced and contrived. For the second time the stooges look uncomfortable playing off of one another. Larry shifting from his and Curly's original role from over ten years ago falls flat! The older film footage actually looks better than the new scenes planted around it. The finale shootout between Sully and Palma is just totally unfunny and a bit distasteful. The scene where Larry and Joe shove pills and liquid medicine down Moe's throat is another disturbing piece of supposed humor. This short fails and its sloppy editing and cheapness become the major focal point. It steals away the action presented on the screen by the actors. But one tends to prefer watching and laughing at the obvious flaws than watching the humorless comedy performed by the stooges and supporting players. Vernon Dent is the only asset and his footage is a staple of the older film. The old stuff outshines the newer stuff by large margins. The funny scenes are so small that you have to look quick to find them. Don't blink or you'll miss them.

The timing is way off and unnatural. This is a very stale humorless short that in my opinion should have never been released. Its running time drags and one can feel the boredom arise out of this very slow, uneven, disjointed, distasteful, poor editing and cheap short that delivers only one thing...hoping that the next film will be a major improvement over this awful stuff!

HORSING AROUND

September 12, 1957

15 minutes.

Directed By: Jules White

With: Harriette Tarler, Emil Sitka and Tony the wonder Horse.

Joe discovers that a champion circus horse is about to be put out to pasture permanently. Their sister Birdie announces that the circus horse in fact the father of her colt. The Stooges and their reincarnated sister rush out to the circus grounds to stop the killing of the circus horse. They all succeed.

A sequel of sorts to their first released short, HOOFS AND GOOFS, HORSING AROUND is mildly entertaining and aims solely for smiles and cuteness. It is a definite improvement over GUNS A POPPIN. Minus the landlord and his daughter (who incidentally plays a showgirl in this particular film) leaves the trio to their own devices to get the laughs. Emil Sitka who appears in his second Joe Besser film has a little bit more to do than he had in SPACE SHIP SAPPY. He is a nearsighted circus horse trainer who is out to put both Larry and Moe who are dressed in a horse costume out to pasture. It is a mildly funny moment.

The film as a whole is an interesting short. The physical humor is less than one might expect from a Stooges comedy. And the idea of following another film by borrowing its internal story settings so early within the year to make a sequel makes one wonder if both films had originally been set to be one single film. It's possible that the studio had planned this as miniature feature as an idea to introduce Joe Besser. Or had the studio thought that what if the entire series of these last 16 shorts were stretched out into three or four reelers. Maybe they were thinking of producing a brand new television sitcom. Whatever these two films if edited right could have been the longest short film created for the stooges and quite possibly It would have been the closest thing that Joe would have done as a feature film while being a member of the stooges.

67

It sure does raise some serious questions in my mind as well as the all popular, what if...? But back to the analysis of this sequel of sorts. What this film did establish once and for all was that Joe was indeed a true member of The Three Stooges. So far the output of shorts with the exception of GUNS A POPPIN, had some real merit in their unique inventiveness and the type of humor they each delivered. 1957 had released a good majority of above average comedies. One bad film in this batch could be forgiven but the following year produced some really bad films and the good ones were measured by the standards set by these first releases but instead of the series rising above the norm they were swallowed by the fair and often uneven distribution of bad outings.

HORSING AROUND quickly wiped out the bad taste of the prior film. And the remaining two reelers for the rest of this year were above the weaker ones that would soon follow. The only thing that keeps this short from being a direct sequel from its predecessor was that in, Hoofs & Goofs that film ended with Joe having dreamt that his sister had died and then had been reincarnated into a horse. In Horsing Around there is no dream sequence, the events unfolding are now very real.

RUSTY ROMEOS

69

October 17, 1957

16 minutes

Directed By: Jules White

With: Connie Cezan.

The Three Stooges are all engaged to the same woman. A fight ensues and after knocking each other around, Joe comes back into the woman's apartment with a rifle and fills her behind with tacks loaded as bullets within the automatic shotgun.

The second refurbishing film, RUSTY ROMEOS is a remake of an earlier Shemp film. Just a notch above being average the film delivers a sharp twist over the original short. The premise is very similar but the ending has the stooges getting the last laugh. The trouble with this film is that it like the first refurbished short in this period tries to be an exact copy of the original. It moves at a fast clip but the short tries to work Joe as another Shemp. The fortunate thing is that this remake doesn't disappoint. Joe Besser seems to aspire instead of shrink within this framework. Both Moe and Larry are on a high energetic charge and the old stock footage is properly edited into this short. So with the tiny second of seeing Shemp in a picture on Connie's end table the story separates itself from the original. It looks fresh and the gags although an almost word for word remake of a previous outing seems to be a bit better.

The hardest thing for any comedian doing a remake of a previous film is trying to separate yourself from your contemporaries. You want to be as original as possible. You want the comedy you are making to be either an equal or better than the earlier original. In this case Joe Besser does hold his own and one can readily associate this remake as a Joe Besser vehicle. But when working in the shadows of other members of the team you are now a major part of has to have a heavy weight on ones shoulders. To rise above and make a film or routine all your own takes a special talent. Joe shows that he indeed has that particular type of talent. Rusty Romeos is a Besser film and the late, great Shemp who Joe replaced has a split second cameo. It was almost like one stooge passing the baton to another stooge.

Some of the funnier scenes involve the Stooges reupholstering a sofa in their apartment. Larry comes up with a quick scheme to speed up the process. He loads an automatic rifle with tacks and in proper aim drills the tacks into the new fabric now placed behind the dilapidated couch. Of course with such a unique weapon, Joe and Larry fighting over who should use it, Moe has his behind shot and filled with the nasty sharp pointers. This comic prop is later used to exact revenge on the, "Jezebel".

The fight scenes with the Stooges fighting amongst themselves is a fast and funny moment, but it is not anything new. However both Moe and Larry have that old familiar spark to their old style of clowning. Joe gets his best laughs off screen when he and Moe are arguing amongst themselves. The idea of Moe reprimanding Joe is in verbal exchanges in the background. So although Joe gets very little punishment on film, he does create an imaginative idea that asks the audience watching this short to imagine seeing Moe giving Joe his just deserts.

So although this is a remake of an earlier Stooges film, the humor intact, a new face replaces the guy with the long black unkempt hair. It doesn't disappoint and that alone speaks high volumes.

OUTER SPACE JITTERS

December 5, 1957

16minutes.

Directed By: Jules White

With: Emil Sitka, Gene Roth, Philip Van Zandt, Dan Blocker, Joe Palma, Harriette Tarler, Diana Darrin and Arline Hunter.

The Three Stooges relate a bedtime story to their children. In the story they arrive on planet with an old eccentric professor and come in contact with two evil aliens, three women who exists on electricity and a mean zombie monster who wants to kill them. After a hefty chase, the Stooges and the professor make a hasty retreat. After telling their story, the babysitter arrives and she is an exact replica of the zombie in their story! The Stooges make their escape through an opened window.

Another swing into Science fiction comedy, this one is just a few short notches below SPACE SHIP SAPPY. Emil Sitka has his biggest role thus far. Dan Blocker who plays the zombie monster would later go on to star in the popular western television series, BONANZA! The supporting cast is a major plus in this short. Most of them are veterans of older Columbia shorts. They along with the stooges spark a refreshing approach to this unique short. Once again the chase scene is just too short! But a tiny bit longer than the scene in A MERRY MIX UP.

The ending with the stooges jumping out of a window and falling several stories down is very poorly directed. Despite the flawed few seconds of a bad ending what has transpired before allows us to overlook this clumsy finish. Another plus in this film is having the bad guys overact. Their high ego aloofness adds a certain charm to the stooges and the physical mayhem they create within the content of the story. It's the fantasy element that makes this short so enduring. It doesn't try to be a comedy with serious undertones. It is a simple and delightful adventure in an easy to follow science fiction comedy. It has no airs.

The last two reeler to be released in 1957 was a short that ended on a high note! It was a throwback to simpler comedies made over twenty some odd years ago. Its theme may be foreign but its comedy is very familiar and one doesn't have to think in order to get a joke. No pretensions it just concentrates on making you smile and then laugh out loud.

One of the things I always loved about The Three Stooges were the chase scenes with the bad guys and monsters that often appeared throughout their twenty four year history in the shorts department. The chase scene in OUTER SPACE JITTERS is clever but it almost seems as though more time and jokes could have been inserted in the fold. Not too say this particular chase scene wasn't good, it was and stands out as the most elaborate one in this period. I just wish that the writers, director and the stooges could have added just a little more of the chase with the zombie.

It was moments like this that in my younger years I recreated within my mind more room for this particular chase scene as well as reconstructing the chase scene in A MERRY MIX UP! The Three Stooges inspired so many different ways on how to rework a familiar sight gag or joke. I can't help but wonder on the influence they sparked in today's new generation of comic actors, writers and directors. Joe Besser having made just a little over a dozen two reelers while being with the stooges must have engineered many ideas of how to do things a bit differently. He knew that in order for his type of child mannerisms to work he had to exercise split second reactions to Moe and Larry. Moe and Larry had to reinvent themselves to fit with the newest member of their trio and for the most part they all succeeded in developing a tight knitted union. The chemistry took a little longer to incorporate itself into the fold but it did arrive! By the end of 1957 Joe Besser was a stooge!

One thing I have to add is that these last 16 shorts had hidden potentials that just went unnoticed. The films could have better constructed comedies. They seemed to miss the mark just a bit slightly. I honestly believe that had the shorts department just taken a bit more concern in the overall quality of these last films that the original ideas presented could have produced some minor comedy classics. Unfortunately they fall some short steps in gaining that higher type of recognition.

But I have noticed that the Besser shorts are being rediscovered and reevaluated. Many have realized that The Three Stooges from this period have been wrongfully misjudged as poor comedies when in fact they had a unique and fresher approach to comedies we see today in this modern time. If one carefully examines the bulk of these films you will discover that they hold up quite well to the insane comedies that dominate our televisions and movie theaters in today's market. While Curly and Shemp are still quite popular in their own ways, the Besser comedies offer combined twists of what made Curly and Shemp so famous. He in a sense sets his own pattern of comic style while making sure we don't forget who came before him. And he gives us a bit of a preview of who is to come afterwards. Besser is the only stooge to incorporate all that the stooges once represented and to instill what was to come a couple of years later.

Emil Sitka as the professor adds a certain spark to this short. He would years later reprise this type of role with bigger and better scenes in the feature film, THE THREE STOOGES IN ORBIT.

1958

Joe Besser second season as a Stooge!

The 1957 output of shorts had been a mix bag of shorts for
The Three Stooges. For the most part, the films despite
their cheapness, gave Joe Besser a warm reception coming

in as an official member of this new Three Stooges set. He had clearly by this point established himself as a stooge.

1958, however offered more disappointments than what the previous year had brought. And the sad truth was that it was only going to get worse. 1958 did produce some interesting concepts, but as a whole these short films became signs of a dying era.

The worst film to emerge out from this year had to be, SWEET AND HOT, in this author's opinion it should have never been made! It was a short that divided the stooges within the framework of a story that just didn't showcase our boys to the best of their advantages as a comedy team. The film looked more like a showcase for actress, Muriel Landers. The Three Stooges were forced to take a giant step back into the shadows.

Another film that divided the Stooges to a much better advantage was FLYING SAUCER DAFFY. Its science fiction theme, taking the popular children's story, CINDERELLA and substituting Joe for the female lead, Moe and Larry as the evil step brothers, reshaping the story into a funny, twisted version of the popular fairytale, gave it a certain charm and became one of the later BESSER comedies most favored by fans.

Unfortunately, FLYING SAUCER DAFFY was the last produced short. Although it would not be the last short released, it was the last film made. Had this film been shelved and released as the final short in 1959, Joe BESSER would have gone out in style as a member of the THREE STOOGES.

It's funny to think that the first year that Joe Besser appeared as a new member of The Three Stooges showed some high potential. Then like an over inflated balloon, one year later, the new thrill had bottomed out. The saddest thing was that Columbia became greedy. They stopped caring about whether a film from their shorts department was funny or just plain out embarrassing. All they cared about at this point was trying to recoup losses. They held on until they had bled the total department dry. Like the three vampires in Space Ship Sappy, the studio sucked the life out of The Three Stooges. Our boys were literally stuck between a rock and a hard place. Their reputation as funny, comedic clowns was being flushed down the toilet. 1958 held very little in giving the stooges a new lease on life. But unbeknownst to all three was that despite the poor quality of shorts now being produced, a new medium was showcasing the older Three Stooges films and slowly but surely, the stooges resurgence was growing and a newer generation of people were beginning to rediscover this unique comedy team. Although they didn't know it at the time, The Three Stooges were going to become more popular than they had been in their earlier heyday. A rebirth had just begun.

QUIZ WHIZZ

February 13, 1958

15minutes.

Directed By: Jules White

With: Greta Thyssen, Gene Roth, Milton Frome, Emil Sitka and Bill Brauer.

Joe wins a sweepstakes contest. He is soon swindled out of his winnings by a couple of con artists. The Stooges go to claim their money won back, but instead are conned into acting as three orphaned children for a man and his lady friend. The boys quickly learn that they are being set up to being murdered. They reverse the tables, subdue the crooks and get their winning sweepstakes check back.

QUIZ WHIZZ is another weak entry. It was not as weak as GUNS A POPPIN but not so far removed from ranking right up there with it. The film has potential and there are some clever gags in isolated spots but for the most part the humor is forced. The gag of Joe sitting on Gene's lap while munching away on a cigar is a very distasteful joke that consumes precious moments that could have been used to create better and funnier sequences. When Greta hits Larry over the head with a bat it seems too real to be funny. It actually presents a very uncomfortable feeling of pain and that kind of reflection from a team that was so accustomed to making pain seem nonexistent kind of helps to mar the funnier moments in this picture. In the very beginning the scene where Moe and Larry panic over a missing Joe seems contrived and forced. It isn't funny but rather embarrassing and the comedy very wooden. It isn't until Joe walks into the room that The Three Stooges for a brief time rise above the staleness of what came before.

This is a on and off comedy short that tries too hard to be funny. Its bad scenes dominate the good ones. For mere brief seconds throughout the film we glimpses of what could have been a very clever and possibly a close contender to one of the better Joe efforts. It just doesn't realize its many obvious flaws. Jules White seemed to really drop the ball on this one.

It's sad when a film that has so many open unrealized potentials fails to deliver consistent humor. The short does move at a fast clip but it stumbles along its path. Just when we think it's going to get better it turns toward being a poorly constructed short. Joe Besser gives his most but even he can't overcome the distasteful cigar scene that makes one want to throw up! It seems to be a cheap trick just in order to fill time. One wishes they would have shortened this particular scene and added something to make us laugh.

When watching these weaker films I often wonder just how the whole editing process really worked. Didn't White preview his finished products? What's even worse is that when a Besser film was bad all the interior flaws become more noticeable. It adds to the weaknesses and creates a very uncomfortable viewing for an audience who wants a pure, simple comedy that won't make them feel sick to their stomachs.

Once again Emil Sitka is regulated to a minor role of that of an IRS agent who comes to the Stooges' apartment in order to collect Uncle Sam's half of the winning dough. He nearly has his head blown off by the Stooges mishandling a firearm. Greta Thyssen makes her debut in this short. Despite her fleeting appearances in only three shorts with The Three Stooges she did become a favorite as a leading lady in the last films of The Three Stooges with Joe Besser.

87

FIFI BLOWS HER TOP

April10, 1958

16minutes.

Directed By: Jules White

With: Vanda Dupre, Philip Van Zandt, Harriette Tarler and Christine McIntyre.

After reminiscing about their wartime sweethearts, Joe discovers that his long lost love lives next door. Now several years later she is married to a man who really wants nothing to do with her. After a domestic mix up when the woman inadvertently locks herself out from her own apartment, the husband comes home and he too is locked out. The Stooges hide the female in an old trunk. Unknowing this the husband announces that he plans to divorce his wife. Upon hearing this the wife pops out of the trunk, knocks her horrible husband out cold and then reunites her lost love for Joe.

FIFI BLOWS HER TOP is a partial remake of an earlier Shemp film. For the most part it comes out as a much funnier comedy. It also borrows from an old Laurel and Hardy film in its second half. Despite its familiar trappings it is a mildly amusing two reeler. The throwback scenes where each stooge recalls a lost love is a fresh approach to moving this story along. The older stock footage adds a certain charm. The stooges as bumbling as ever deliver some interesting set pieces. The final half is worked as if it is the first time being played. The two main supporting players add to the comedies personal value. It comes off fresh and original even though it is a repeat of two earlier films.

FIFI BLOWS HER TOP is a few notches above being average. It is one of the better comedies produced during this awkward period. Joe Besser is in top form and his integrated comedy with his two partners is a very pleasing experience to view. Larry has pretty much the bulk of the physical comedy and he gives it his all! Moe is a bit stifled but he comes off pretty pleasing as well. There is something about this film that invites the viewer into its simplicity. One after watching this film can't help but think about it and have an urgent sense to review it all over again! And that's an amazing quality of a good comedy film. It moves at a natural fast and funny pace. It's just a simple bag of tricks that works on the viewer creating a sense of feeling superior to the stooges on screen.

Now I earlier listed this film in a category of mildly entertaining shorts and I still hold up on that. But out of that list this one definitely shines as the greater of that list. It could be considered an almost original Besser but in truth it is a remake of two earlier shorts. Not that it deserves to be shot down. The stooges in this film put an electric energy into their comedy and it does shine through. Joe Besser once again doing a partial remake of a Shemp film comes off just a tiny bit better. It seemed out of all the refurbishing's that he could better replace Shemp than he could Curly. How ironic since he resembled Curly in a physical form than Shemp. And his mannerisms were more childlike compared to the salty Shemp.

Now don't mistake that I am doing a comparison of who was better, because I am not. What I'm trying to point out is that the stories that had originally been written with Shemp in mind also work with Joe. Two completely different set of middle stooges who seem to work well in

90

similar story settings. Joe is radically different from Shemp but he seems to fit quite well in a film that Shemp had already done. Joe not imitating Shemp but using his own character traits actually compliments the refurbished product. Maybe because Joe on one hand knew he had to reinvent his character that his predecessor had already done so that he came off entirely different and on the other hand being forced to rework an older film he had to make sure that this particular project didn't remind people that it had already been done just a few short years ago.

To a much larger degree this film is in a sense an original Joe Besser short. Despite the brief older stock footage in the earliest scenes, once Joe begins remembering his lost romance the short does become despite borrowing from other long ago comedies, an almost original Stooges' comedy two reeler. The formula goes way back to the silent era of comedy. It was done by Laurel and Hardy as well as several other comics. Sometimes old material if recruited and done right can be just as funny as from the original. This particular storyline derived from early burlesque skits doesn't disappoint. The comedy almost comes off being new.

PIES AND GUYS

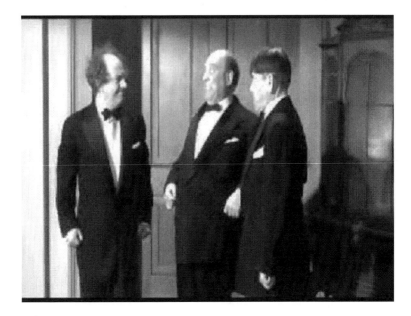

June12, 1958

16minutes.

Directed By: Jules White.

With: Greta Thyssen, Milton Frome, Gene Roth, Emil Sitka, Harriette Tarler, Helen Dickson, Symona Boniface, Barbara Slater and Al Thompson.

The Three Stooges are inept plumbers recruited by high society on a bet that they can be transformed into gentlemen. When the experiment seems to be going well, a pie is thrown and the Stooges revert back to their original Moran's mental capacity and pretty soon an all-out pie fight ensues.

In this third Stooge adaptation of Pygmalion, the trio are repairmen who make a scene in the presence of two psychologists, Professors Quackenbush and Sedletz. Quackenbush makes a bet with Sedletz that he can turn the boys into gentlemen through environment. Training is slow and painful for the professor, who pulls his hair out in disgust. However, the Stooges do have the opportunity to flirt with the professor's assistant, while learning table etiquette. Finally, the Stooges will decide the wager by their behavior at a fancy society party.

Naturally, the party goes awry. Joe greets the Countess Spritzwasser by kissing her hand, and biting off the diamond in her ring. Realizing this, Moe and Larry take Joe to a secluded area to lecture him, only to find he has swiped a load of silverware.

Joe then grabs a pie from a pastry table, and tries to eat it whole. Moe sees this, swipes the pie, and pushes Joe out of the way. Seeing another guest, Mrs. Smythe-Smythe (Symona Boniface, in archival footage), approaching, Moe tosses the pie straight up —to which it attaches itself to the ceiling. Seeing that he can barely get a sentence out, she sympathetically comments, "Young man, you act as if you have the Sword of

Damocles hanging over your head." Moe replies that Mrs. Smythe-Smythe is a psychic and flees, to which the pie comes crashing down on the society matron. This sparks off a massive pie melee that takes no prisoners.

When a comedian is handed the task of imitating another comic, forced to repeat an older film and having his own individual character stifled he rarely comes off as anything but a mere copycat. This unfortunately is the case in this two reeler with Joe. It's not an entirely bad film but it gives Joe a rather sad showcase for his own individual style of humor. His second Curly refurbishing is way better than the first one he did. But as a whole one is looking for Curly! Joe Besser isn't Curly. It's a shame that Jules White didn't allow Joe to be his natural funny self! It makes this two reeler just an average outing.

Besser as pointed out before was a gifted comedian. His humor if it was carefully watched and built into the stooges' old bag of tricks it worked marvelously. He was a stooge but he wasn't Curly and this film insults him by asking viewers to compare the two. It's not fair for Curly or Joe! But despite this major misgiving PIES AND GUYS is a fast moving two reeler. It is the above reasoning that puts it in the mildly entertaining category. Another fault this film has is the overabundance of old stock footage. Not only has Joe been robbed of being himself he is overshadowed by the older film. Moe and Larry come out better because they are not forced to imitate anyone but themselves.

You would think that Joe would fit perfectly in replacing Curly in his original role, but as mentioned before in my other reviews, Joe comes off better replacing Shemp than he does Curly.

Emil Sitka repeats his familiar role of butler. Greta Thyssen in her second Stooges' comedy comes off a little better than she had in QUIZ WHIZ. In her first two shorts she gets clobbered by sticky, creamy cakes and pies.

SWEET AND HOT

September 4, 1958.

16minutes.

Directed By: Jules White.

With: Muriel Landers.

Moe is a psychiatrist who tries to break Joe and Larry's niece of stage fright.

Small town boy made good, producer Larry returns to his home farm town. There he hears and watches as his friends Joe and sister Tiny (Muriel Landers) working on their farm. Talented Tiny is singing. After hearing her, Larry asks them to join his New York nightclub act. But Tiny has a fear of performing in front of a live audience, so Larry and Joe take Tiny to a German psychiatrist (Moe), who uses hypnosis to take Tiny back to the childhood origin of her problem.

At the psychiatrist's office, Tiny, under hypnosis, reveals that she has been scared since an incident in her family's barn. She was singing and pretend playing on a piano in front of her father (Moe) when her uncles (Larry and Joe)

100

come inside to listen to her singing and applaud when she finishes. Moe demands she sings more for them. Tiny refuses and hides in fear. After being scared again, the psychiatrist convinces a hypnotized Tiny that she should sing because people love hearing her sing. Tiny agrees and is cured of her fear. She becomes a professional singer, making her debut onstage with Joe and Larry. Tiny sings while Larry plays a violin and Joe dances.

This is undoubtedly the worse Besser film in this whole series of two reelers! I'll give it marks for it being original but that's pretty much all I'll give it! It strays so far from being a Three Stooges comedy one has to wonder why it was ever made. There is nothing funny or inspiring about this film. It is a very hard short to watch! Moe has the task of playing two separate unfunny roles. The Three Stooges are divided within this framework. Joe and Larry are pretty much regulated to the background. Muriel Landers dominates the entire film and she like the rest is very unfunny! Let's go onto the next review...

FLYING SAUCER DAFFY

October9, 1958.

16minutes.

Directed By: Jules White.

With: Gail Bonney, Emil Sitka, Bek Nelson, Diana Darrin, Harriette Tarler and Joe Palma.

Joe's accidental snapshot of a paper plate blown by a breeze, is mistaken for a picture of a UFO. However, Moe and Larry take the credit for the photo, and are paid a huge sum. Angered, Joe leaves the boys for a camping trip, only to meet two genuine and beautiful aliens from Planet Zircon who allow Joe to photograph them. Moe and Larry end up arrested when their UFO picture is revealed to be a fraud. They are put in straitjackets and incarcerated in a psychiatric hospital while Joe becomes a national hero.

The last trip into Science Fiction with Joe Besser as a stooge is a high average outing. Like the film before the stooges are split within the film. But unlike that film before, this is a clever reworking of Cinderella! This short has humor and a very well-constructed story. Joe who plays a male version of Cinderella is in top form. The contrast between him and Moe and Larry is beautifully played to the hilt. All the supporting players help this film move at a brisk pace. What's more compared to most of the previous shorts it doesn't look cheap! It seems that Jules White took a little extra attention in making this a superior product. Maybe because this was the last Three Stooges film to be produced.(but not the last one released) It shines over the last batch of shorts released earlier in 1958.

This also marks the last original comedy produced in this period. The last remaining three were remakes of earlier Curly and Shemp films. If this had been Joe's swan song as part of The Three Stooges it's very possible that he might have been reevaluated as a later member of the team. It's sad that just half a dozen Besser films shine throughout all of these 16 shorts. If Besser had made maybe half a dozen more original comedies instead of being handed the thankless task of filling in on the remakes he might have climbed out of medium shorts and really paved a path so far removed from being saddled with improving on already classic films that didn't need to be reused. Out of all the stooges Besser in my personal opinion had to rise forcefully out from his two contemporaries by trying to improve on material that really didn't need to be touched. In the two years that he was a stooge finding his own way had to be a difficult chore. Unlike Curly Joe Derita who followed after him, he didn't have the fullest opportunity to be considered a real original adding to the act. But Besser did prevail. When the short was right he came through with high earned honors of creating some memorable comedy. If he had stayed on just a bit longer, maybe appeared with Moe and Larry in a feature film whether starring or just cast as simple comedy relief it's highly possible that his contributions as a full fledge member of this trio might have vanished the comparisons between Curly and Shemp.

FLYING SAUCER DAFFY has also some unique studio outdoor shots that help this comedy move at its brisk pace. The interior shots of the apartment are cheap looking, but one can almost over look this tiny flaw. The short as a whole has so much charm and childlike innocence. Joe Besser and his naturally funny characteristic traits are what adds to the humor. We feel for Joe. Both Moe and Larry as the stepbrothers are quite convincing in their mean roles. The final jail scene with both Moe and Larry wrapped in strait jackets serves as a nice close out gag.

Emil Sitka appears here in his last two reeler with The Three Stooges.

106

OILS WELL THAT ENDS WELL

December 4, 1958.

16minutes.

Directed By: Jules White.

The Stooges have lost their jobs. Adding insult to injury, they received a letter from Dad with the news that he requires surgery. To help pay for the operation, the father suggests the boys search for uranium on his mining property. The boys locate the uranium, but run afoul of a load of dynamite. Then, when they are trying to fix the water pump, it starts gushing oil. Joe tries to cork it by sitting on it, but he is sent flying into the air. When he wishes it would stop, it does, much to Moe and Larry's dismay. Joe manages to get the oil started again, and the boys are in the money.

Another Curly remake but unlike the other two this one allows Joe Besser to move in his own style of humor. The Three Stooges are the only players in this short. It starts off just a tiny bit on the slow side but quickly picks up in its pacing. The editing is slightly above average and as a whole this film comes off better than any of the other remakes. Joe Besser has several laugh out loud moments and being that this short is basically a string of gags and verbal insults and the fact that the only stars in this film are the stooges moves this short at a nice enjoyable speed. It is the last great Besser film.

The sight gags and physical comedy is really not anything that we haven't seen before, but the energy is fresh and the outdoor scenes produce some genuine funny moments. The cabin scene where the boys get ready for bed is pure hilarious. The old stock footage used in this short actually enhances the action. The rousing comic final is a perfect fitting to everything that has proceeded it. Although a remake, Joe takes sole ownership of this two reeler. He doesn't allow his comedy to be compared to other middle stooges. Larry and Moe are at their most sparkling performances. This undiluted Three Stooges comedy ranks right up with the better original output of Besser shorts.

This is the only refurbished product that strays from the average other films remade. It is a perfect and very rare showcase for this new Three Stooges. It is a treasured keepsake that had this been the only film made with Besser as a stooge it would have sparked a sincere wondering of how he would have made it as a member of The Three Stooges. We already know how he would have done! The only thing really missing is why there couldn't have been more Besser short films?! Why did Columbia waste our time in having someone double for a dead Shemp (no disrespect intended) when we could have had four more Besser films to watch. 20 instead of 16 would have been an extra time of enjoying a truly gifted comic genius!

I love Shemp! I love Curly! I love Joe! I love them all! It's time that we stop the comparisons and appreciate what Besser brought into the whole fold of things. He deserves to be recognized for his own contributions as one of The Three Stooges. It is not his fault that these last two reelers were cheaply made or poorly directed or poorly edited! Besser, Fine and Howard did show a movie going public that The Three Stooges could still carry on despite some tragic setbacks!

Here more than anything is a situation comedy that despite being filmed in glorious black and white fits well enough into the situation comedies shown today on television. Another plus is that the editing is pretty tight and the older footage is nicely matched to the new recorded footage. It may not be an original, but it sure does make an audience forget where this two reeler originated from.

1959

The final two films featuring Joe Besser as a Stooge.

1959 was the last year we would see Joe Besser as a member of The Three Stooges. Two more films would be released, TRIPLE CROSSED and SAPPY BULL FIGHTERS, ended the Besser era. The next stooge, CURLY JOE DERITA.

It was another period of transition. Although the truth of the matter was that Joe Besser had already left the act over a year ago. These last two shorts had been produced in 1957 and held back until 1959. SAPPY BULL FIGHTERS was the better of the two final films released. Despite its sloppy editing and failing to match the famous bull ride with the older footage from WHAT'S A MATADOR, the film had some worthwhile merits. The interaction between the stooges seemed sharper and more established than some of the prior films, unfortunately it became a very sad farewell.

Just as audiences had warmed up to Besser being a stooge, they were in less than two months after the final two reeler had been distributed, introduced to a brand new middle stooge. But Besser had paved the road for Derita and he had been the first to explore outer space, aim his comedy at a children's point of view, help to begin toning down the violence in the films and even introduce some interesting changes among the stooges. Many ideas emerged during the Besser period, although most didn't continue, they tried to introduce a different approach to the usual standards of stooges' formulas. It had been a unique, fresh and quite often radical attempt in changing the regular styles already established by Curly and Shemp.

Joe Besser had forged his own brand of comedy into being a member of the stooges and despite the obvious setbacks, he managed to come out making a great impression and he and Moe and Larry made a memorable trio of clowns.

The Three Stooges for a brief short while were, JOE BESSER, MOE HOWARD & LARRY FINE! They made us laugh and created some memorable classic, isolated hilarious moments. I believe that Besser made his greatest mark in show business when he became a member of The Three Stooges. It is the most we see and hear about Joe Besser. (Although his appearance as Stinky on The Abbott & Costello show, follows a close second.) I am so glad that Columbia released the entire bulk of all the Three Stooges 198 short films, plus some rare shorts that featured Joe Besser, Shemp Howard & Joe Derita in their own starring two reelers before they ever became members of the famous trio. The last volume of films in this DVD collection is a must have and see if you are a Joe Besser fan and are curious in learning more about the comic and his individual style of humor.

114

TRIPLE CROSSED

February 2, 1959.

15minutes.

Directed By: Jules White.

With: Angela Stevens, Mary Ainslee, Diana Darrin, Connie Cezan and Johnny Kascier.

Larry is a womanizer who is having an affair with Moe's wife Belle. At the same time, he is also making eyes at Joe's fiancée, Millie. However, Moe tracks down the conniving Larry at his pet shop, and gives him the works before Larry calms him down. Realizing he needs to cover his tracks, Larry looks for a "fall guy" in the form of Joe. Larry then gets Joe a job as an underwear salesman and the first place he goes is Moe's home.

While Joe is modeling his ware, Larry lies to Moe about Joe's advances on Millie. Both of them go storming over to Moe's, while Joe flees up the chimney. After making a quiet getaway, Joe bumps into Larry, and turns him in.

1959 was the last time we would see Joe Besser as a member of The Three Stooges. Two months after the release of his last two reeler a new stooge would be introduced. Two short films were all that was left and unfortunately they were far from being the best produced. TRIPLE CROSSED is a remake of yet another Shemp film. It also would be the last short to separate the boys within the film. It may not be their worst outing but it sure does ride on the heels of the worst Besser films. It sadly banishes any originality from the original film. It tries to make Joe into a Shemp. What it does instead is create an uncomfortable reminder of what had come before. This short although it does have some laughable rare moments it is once again a forced and contrived setting.

Once again the editing is poor and although Shemp is long gone the older stock footage haunts us with brief seconds of his hand coming out from the chimney and his screams of pain when Moe fires his gun up into the chimney. Larry plays a perfect louse but he doesn't come off as being funny. It is Moe and Joe who handle the short funny moments and sadly Moe's funniest scenes are carried over from the older footage. It was interesting when the writers tried a different approach to the stooges' usual brand of slapstick, but very rarely did it produce anything funny.

The films ending is stale and both Larry and Moe lack the initial energy to overcome the major flaws in this short. Joe is once again held back from being his natural funny self. He tries but it just isn't authentic. He seems out of his element. In the whole truth this entire film is way out of its element. Maybe if the editing had been tighter, the stock footage lessened, the action more energetic, the humor more prevalent this could have possibly gone down as a mildly good comedy short.

Maybe adding Emil Sitka and Greta Thyssen would have lifted this poor film from being so off the wall unfunny.

118

SAPPY BULL FIGHTERS

June4, 1959.

15minutes.

Directed By: Jules White.

With: Greta Thyssen, George Lewis, Joe Palma, Eddie Laughton and Cy Schindell.

The Stooges are vaudeville entertainers who trek to Mexico to perform their gag bull fight shtick, with Joe as the brave matador, and Moe and Larry dressed in a bull costume. Unfortunately, their gig is cancelled once they arrive, leaving them stranded. Feeling bad for them, attractive señorita Greta gets the boys a gig at the local bull ring. Joe is so ecstatic that he plants a kiss right on Greta's cheek, much to the chagrin of her evil man-hating jealous husband José.

In an act of revenge, José pays the bullring attendant to release a live bull into the ring. Moe and Larry flee the ring, but Joe is unaware of the switch. He eventually head-butts the wild animal, and is paraded out of the ring to the rousing cheers of "Olé, Americano!"

The last Besser film is better than the previous short. It is a remake of a Curly classic. Despite its many merits it falls a little flat. The scene of Joe riding the bull pales compared to the older footage of curly riding the bull. It looks stale and slow moving to the faster and wilder action it tries to imitate. This one isolated scene keeps this film from receiving a higher mark. What comes before and after it is pretty funny stuff. Not entirely a bad swan song for Besser but it's amazing how one tiny spot in a film can destroy the overall quality. If one can easily look past this flaw then one can appreciate that this short doesn't deliberately try to fail. The stooges tangling with a jealous husband is genuine humor and it moves quite rapidly. The stooges in their own spaces deliver vibrant hilarious comedy. But again it comes to a dead halt when the main action of the film doesn't match the older footage and it deliberately shows how cheap the newer footage is in comparison.

SAPPY BULL FIGHTERS is a pleasant outing but it is also disjointed. The studio had to see that this middle part which connects the beginning and ending was way off in its timing. A comedy that could have been given a higher rating is seriously beaten down by sloppy editing. It just is so sad that this last film was so uneven in delivering what should have been a top rated short. Being a remake is one thing but not knowing how to stitch the most important part of a story into the right slot is just very cold and heartless! The Three Stooges deserved better than that!

Greta Thyssen who appears in her last Three Stooges short film does come off way better than her other two film appearances. It just bothers me that this could have been a bright and fast moving two reeler if the editing department would have seriously reviewed the middle part of the film. How this could had gone totally unnoticed?

121

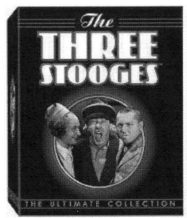
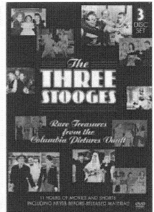
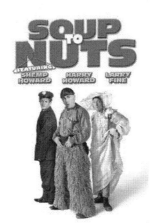

Larry, Moe &
Curly Joe!

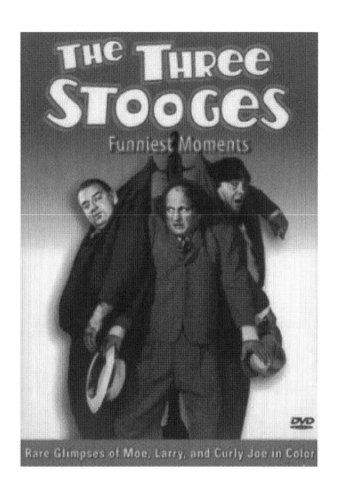

INTRODUCTION:

Here it is! A look at The Three Stooges in their last seven starring movies made in the 1960s. Take a wild, slap in the face, eye poking, head bonking look at The Three Stooges who were riding a new surge of popularity after twenty four years of making two reeler short comedies, they were now starring in their own short series of funny movies.

I am going to review just their seven starring films that featured Curly Joe as the new middle stooge at this particular period of time. This was the final run for these clowns. They came in with a big bang when they arrived at the Columbia shorts department in 1934. The trio consisted at first, Curly Howard, Moe Howard and Larry Fine, who for the next twelve years would entertain movie audiences with their outrageous brand of wild slapstick antics.

Then a new set of stooges arrived in 1947, Shemp Howard replaced Curly. Another unique batch of funny, but radically different type of films continued the familiar tradition of clowning around for another decade. Then Joe Besser replaced Shemp for the last two years that these short comedies had been produced. The last two reel comedy was released in June of 1959.

Two months later, a new guy replaced Joe Besser, his name, Curly Joe Derita. Technically, Mr. Derita had already been inducted into the trio in 1958, but his first starring vehicle as a stooge followed behind the heels of Besser's last short comedy, SAPPY BULL FIGHTERS. The Three

125

Stooges had been enjoying a brand new surge in their popularity when Columbia began releasing their older two reelers to the television market across the nation in the late 1950s.

The comedy had somewhat changed. The violence that had been prevalent in their earlier films had been toned down in their newer feature films. The stooges were also now men in their sixties and although they had a brand new spark in their act, they couldn't deliver the same physical comedy as they had done over three decades ago. Now their comedy focused on a younger generation of viewers who were for the first time rediscovering The Three Stooges.

On the television sets they were introduced to Curly and Shemp! On the big screen, Joe Besser was still appearing in the last of the 16 two reelers! Also Curly Joe had started appearing with Moe and Larry as guest stars on many popular comedy variety shows during the late 50s. It seemed everywhere you looked The Three Stooges were right smack in your face making you laugh.

Here is how I plan to set this book up, first an analyzing of the stooges with Curly Joe and the years they worked together. Then analyzing their starring feature films.

This new book will also feature more pictures. Hope you enjoy KNUCKLE HEADS.

Analyzing Curly- Joe

On December20, 1957, Columbia studios let The Three
Stooges go. They had just finished making, FLYING SAUCER
DAFFY. Although this had been the last two Reeler
completed by the studio, there were still several two
reelers held out from release. Those last films were

127

shelved and released throughout 1958 and 1959. At the end of their twenty four years of making short two reel comedies, the stooges were for the first time out of a job.

So The Three Stooges had decided to go out on tour, but Joe Besser for personal reasons had to quit the act. Both Moe and Larry at this point seriously contemplated ending the team. But as fate would have it the studio they had been previously employed under decided to distribute their older two reel comedies featuring Curly and Shemp Howard, to the semi new medium called television! Almost overnight The Three Stooges popularity soured to new heights.

Moe and Larry came out from their brief semi-retirement, hired Joe Derita as a new stooge and began taking to the road this newest assembly of stooges across the country. Joe Derita adopted Curly Joe as his new name, and soon after reinventing, repolishing, reestablishing themselves, The Three Stooges were back on track.

In 1958, The Three Stooges were invited to appear on a variety of television shows, commercials and personal tours. Norman Maurer, Moe's son-in-law, became the team's new manager. With this sudden surge of renewed popularity it was inevitable that contracts for making new motion pictures starring the stooges were bound to emerge.

Ironically, Columbia the studio that had fired them, invited them to come back and make a feature film. The film, HAVE ROCKET, WILL TRAVEL, followed the last released short, SAPPY BULL FIGHTERS, two months later. It turned out to be a huge commercial as well as audience approved success! The Three Stooges were now in demand for making more movies, appearing on television and having their images used to promote a huge variety of commercial products.

The 1960s had breathed a new life into a classic comedy team. For this entire decade the stooges were a constant in the minds of their public as well as in the minds of their critics. They had burned themselves like branding irons into the social status and history that forever would define a small part of what the sixties were all about. They among other topics of this era became a symbol of sorts. They now held onto what slapstick comedy had once been. They became the main representatives of a time long ago gone. They helped in a very large way of keeping the fire burning.

Curly Joe Derita had the physical appearance of looking like an older Curly Howard. Now like his predecessors he never tried to be anyone but himself. He instilled his own brand of humor into the stooges. He made himself an identifiable, individual member who brought his own unique style of comedy into the fold of being a stooge.

Unlike Joe Besser, who he had replaced, but like Curly and Shemp Howard, he had the golden opportunity of previewing his new role on stages and television. He had the advantage of testing out what worked and what didn't. He wasn't just placed into the group on short notice. He managed to work himself into the comedy already established by the stooges. His chemistry was developed and fine-tuned and in a short time all three men were fully recognized as The Three Stooges.

The starring feature films for the most part were aimed primarily for kiddie audiences who were their biggest fans. But looking back at those movies from the 1960s, they entertained all age groups. That's a huge thing to accomplish! Granted these films are pretty simple in their construction but their overall charms, slapstick comedy, verbal one liners have provoked tons of hilarious laughter.

But like Joe Besser, maybe to a level of a smaller degree, Derita has had his share of people who have compared him to Curly and Shemp. These people don't like him. That's such a shame! Curly Joe Derita tried to break out of being compared to the members that had come before him. This was an obstacle that at times came to be very burdensome, especially when television was constantly rerunning the Columbia shorts that featured Curly or Shemp. Pretty soon People started dividing themselves into separated groups of who they wanted to choose to be a representative of the real Three Stooges. It also didn't help matters when this new set of stooges were asked to host the older versions of the shorts from thirty years ago. Despite this, Derita forged his own way and truly created a memorable stooge that for the most part made most people realize that he could carry his own individualism and be fully recognized as The Three Stooges of the 1960s.

Now out of the seven films I'm highlighting in this unique book, my personal favorites are, HAVE ROCKET, WILL TRAVEL, THREE STOOGES GO AROUND THE WORLD IN A DAZE and OUTLAWS IS A COMING. I love all the films, but these three in my personal opinion are the funnier ones out of this entire bunch.

The saddest film unfortunately in this group, SNOW WHITE AND THE THREE STOOGES. It has potential but it fails to give us the stooges we have come to love and laugh at. They are basically relegated to the background. The opening credits are the closest thing in seeing our boys in their natural comedy. It's a sad preview to what should have been a better film as a whole. But it really doesn't deserve all the negativity that has followed it throughout the years.

Despite the stooges being men in their sixties, they still managed to be incredibly hilarious. They continued to create and recreate their special brand of humor. Norman Maurer as their personal manager stirred the team into a very profitable enterprise. He helped in establishing their personal importance in whatever project they were assigned to do. He took pride and care in continuing their popularity among their fans and people who at one time or another didn't see what was as important in their longevity as a comedy team.

They lasted as long as they did because they were funny. They worked hard and throughout the many transitions that often plagued the team, they prevailed. They made some heavy sacrifices and suffered unrepairable damages that in most cases amongst other popular comedy teams would have permanently crippled a successful career. It took a lot of self-endurance, reinventing and pushing hard through some turbulent weather and just not giving up that gave The Three Stooges their long, long life.

HAVE ROCKET, WILL TRAVEL

AUGUST, 1959.

RUNNING TIME: 1hour, 16minutes.

DIRECTOR: David Lowell Rich.

STUDIO: Columbia.

WITH: Jerome Cowan, Anna Lisa, Bob Colbert, Marjorie Bennett, Don Lamond, Nadine Ducas, Robert J. Stevenson and Del McKennon.

Have Rocket, Will Travel is a 1959 American science fiction comedy film starring The Three Stooges. By this time, the trio consisted of Moe Howard, Larry Fine, and new "third Stooge" Joe Derita (dubbed "Curly Joe"). Released by Columbia Pictures, the feature was produced to capitalize on the comedy trio's late 1950s resurgence in popularity.

The Stooges are janitors working at a space center who accidentally blast off to Venus. They encounter a talking unicorn, a giant fire breathing tarantula, and an alien computer who has destroyed all human life on the planet and creates three evil duplicates of the Stooges. When the boys return home triumphant, they are given a hero's welcome.

Two months after releasing the final Three Stooges short film, SAPPY BULL FIGHTERS, Columbia released, HAVE ROCKET, WILL TRAVEL. The film marked a new beginning for The Three Stooges. A new middle stooge was once again thrown into the mix. Curly Joe Derita had officially established himself as a new stooge. This also marked the last time that the boys would employ their last eye poke.

HAVE ROCKET, WILL TRAVEL is a fine introductory feature film that doesn't waste time in establishing its plot. It introduces the stooges in a very familiar setting, all three in bed sleeping and snoring. The stooges are at their most energetic humor. The gags flow natural and funny. The pace of the film moves at a fast and brisk speed.

The chemistry created among the stooges makes it seem as though Curly Joe had already been a lifelong member. Their interactions with one another are brilliantly blended. Director David Lowell Rich who had never worked with the stooges seems to rise above the occasion and churns out an incredibly well made low budget comedy.

Jerome Cowan who plays the boys nemesis is in fine casting and creates a marvelous foil in which the boys play off of. Anna Lisa and Bob Colbert play their corny romance sub plot to the fullest in creating a laughable love couple. The film in a sense makes fun of itself and older comedy films that dominated the 30s and 40s. They play these certain older elements for laughs and for nothing more or less.

One of the many films highlights come when the stooges meet their robotic doubles. The clever special effects and chase scene is built to create a wild rumpus chaotic comedy of mix ups and funny run INS with some clever old stooges routines and one liners thrown into the fold. It a science fiction remake of sorts of the earlier short film, A MERRY MIX UP.

It also serves as a set up for the films funny ending. The later party, pie throwing, slapping melee situation wraps the film up quite nicely and presents another pleasant throwback into what comedy films once represented.

So you have a healthy dose of wild old fashioned comedy mixed with science fiction, the blend of both is pleasing and very amusing. The film knows it is a low budget comedy and it does nothing to hide that fact. It doesn't put on any false airs. It may not be a comedy classic, but it comes mighty close in gaining that type of recognition.

SNOW WHITE AND THE THREE STOOGES

RELEASED: June, 1961.

RUNNING TIME: 1hour, 47minutes.

DIRECTOR: Walter Lang.

STUDIO: Twentieth-Century Fox.

WITH: Carol Heiss, Edson Stroll, Patricia Medina, Guy Rolfe, Michael David, Buddy Baer, Edgar Barrier, Peter Cole, Lisa Mitchell, Chuck Lacey, Owen McGivney, Gloria Doggett, Leon McNabb, Blossom Rock, Leslie Farrell, Craig Cooke, Burt Mustin, Richard Collier, Herbie Faye and Edward Innes.

Snow White and the Three Stooges is the second feature film to star the Three Stooges after their 1959 resurgence in popularity. By this time, the trio consisted of Moe Howard, Larry Fine, and Joe Derita (dubbed "Curly Joe"). Released by 20th Century Fox, this was the trio's take on the classic fairy tale Snow White and the Seven Dwarfs. The film was retitled Snow White and the Three Clowns in Great Britain.

Olympic gold medalist figure skater Carol Heiss starred as Snow White, who must flee her home after her stepmother wishes her to be dead. Seeking refuge in the cottage of the seven dwarfs, she accidentally meets the Stooges, who are house sitting for them while they are away.

Once upon a time, in the kingdom of Fortunio, a noble king and his lovely young queen lack but one blessing to make their joy complete. The queen gives birth to a daughter named Snow White, but dies soon after. The king mourns her, but in time, he remarries because of the pleading of his people. His new Queen is a beautiful, but evil woman who soon becomes jealous of Snow White's beauty.

On her 17th birthday, Snow White's father dies and the wicked queen immediately imprisons her. Eventually, the queen's jealousy of her stepdaughter becomes so great that she orders her killed. Snow White escapes her hired assassin and finds refuge in the empty cottage of the seven dwarfs, soon to be joined by the Three Stooges, who are traveling to the castle with their ward Quarto. But the boy they have raised since childhood (also narrowly escaping an assassination attempt by the queen) is in reality Prince Charming, who though he has lost his memory, is betrothed to Snow White.

Snow White and the Prince fall in love, but the queen has him kidnapped when she suspects his true identity. The Stooges, disguised as cooks, attempt to rescue him, but he falls from a staircase in the palace and is presumed dead. Meanwhile, the queen learns from her magic mirror that Snow White is still alive. With the help of her magician, Count Olga, she transforms herself into a witch and succeeds in getting Snow White to take a bite from a poisoned apple.

As she rides back to the palace, she encounters the Stooges, and thanks to an inadvertent wish they make on

140

a magic sword (stolen from Count Olga), she crashes her broom into a mountainside and falls to her death. The Stooges then find the poisoned Snow White, but they do not bury her. Instead, they place her on a bed, and pray to her each day.

Meanwhile, the Prince (Quarto) has not died from his fall. Instead, he is saved by a group of men who want to revolt against the Evil Queen's rule over Fortunio. As the prince recovers, he realizes that his memory has returned, and so he knows that he is indeed a Prince, and that Snow White is the princess he was destined to marry.

After leading a successful revolt which places him on the throne of Fortunio, the prince sends out searchers to find Snow White and the Stooges, unaware that, thanks to yet another inadvertent wish on Count Olga's sword, they are no longer in the country of Fortunio. All searches are fruitless, and Prince Charming is close to giving up hope when he learns of the Evil Queen's magic mirror. The mirror responds truthfully to the desperate Prince's pleas, and the Prince sets off on his journey. He arrives at the Stooges' cabin just in time to dispel the effects of the poisoned apple. Snow White and Prince Charming are married and live happily ever after.

Moe Howard referred this film as a Technicolor mistake. The Three Stooges who receive second Billing are regulated into a supporting role. Their humor is way toned down to the point that their comedy is unrecognizable!

141

They are a comedy team subdued. It is sad because had another director took the helm and really incorporated the familiar comedy that is tradition by the stooges this film as a whole could have emerged as a genuine comedy classic.

Walter Lang who was a competent director just didn't bother making The Three Stooges a major part of his work. He almost seemed to shun them. This film went over budget and unfortunately despite its handsome production values, almost flawless fight scenes, and elaborate settings this film hadn't realized that the audiences seeing The Three Stooges name in the title, expected to see them as funny clowns instead of unfunny character actors.

The studio trying to build an up and coming Olympic athlete into a star, Carol Heiss, didn't bother to realize that a film with The Three Stooges in it carried some weight and could've helped build this into a respectable comedy, adventure, fantasy film. You don't place a potential star in a picture that kills its main attraction.

The fairytale opening credits give The Three Stooges their only brief, shining moment. It is the only comic highlight that comes way too soon and promises a potentially funny premise and then suddenly goes into over serious mode. The opening lies to the audience watching and deliberately throws their trust down the drain. Many people were so distraught over how the stooges had been handled offered some really negative, nasty comments that in the short

142

run damaged the big budget picture to fail miserably at the box office.

Looking at the film today, one can see potential that just wasn't realized. The Three Stooges had been in their first and only dud. Which when you think about it, it's not such a bad thing. For the record they quickly rose over this and continued being a big name celebrity comedy team! But the film however did kill the career of its star, wannabe, Carol Heiss.

144

THE THREE STOOGES MEET HERCULES

RELEASED: January, 1962.

RUNNING TIME: 1hour, 28minutes.

DIRECTOR: Edward Bernds.

STUDIO: Columbia.

WITH: Vicky Trickett, Quin Redeker, George N. Neise, Samson Burke, Mike McKeever, Marlin McKeever, Emil Sitka, Hal Smith, John Cliff, Lewis Charles, Barbara Hines, Terry Huntingdon, Diana Piper, Gregg Martell, Gene Roth, Edward Foster, Cecil Elliot and Rusty Wescoatt.

The Three Stooges Meet Hercules is the third feature film to star the Three Stooges after their 1959 resurgence in popularity. By this time, the trio consisted of Moe Howard, Larry Fine, and Joe Derita (dubbed "Curly Joe"). Released by Columbia Pictures, The Three Stooges Meet Hercules was directed by long-time Stooge director Edward Bernds. This was the most financially successful of the Stooges' feature films.

The Stooges work at Dismal's Drug Store in Ithaca, New York, where they befriend Schuyler Davis (Quinn Redeker), and the owner of the shop next door, who is attempting to build a time machine. With the boys' "help", the machine transports the boys, Schuyler and disaffected girlfriend Diane Quigley (Vicki Trickett) back in time to Ithaca in ancient Greece during the reign of the lecherous King

146

Odius (George N. Neise). The King, after defeating and imprisoning Ulysses because the Stooges are believed to be gods, has a yearning for Diane. Realizing they have disrupted the proper course of history, Schuyler and the boys free Ulysses, after which Odius banishes them to the galleys, where Schuyler builds impressive muscles while constantly rowing.

After an escape and shipwreck, they kill a monster with the help of Joe's sleeping pills and start billing Schuyler as Hercules at a local gladiatorial arena. The real Hercules (Samson Burke) gets wind of their game and confronts them, but after single combat the Stooges convince Hercules to help them rescue Diane in a chariot chase. The time travelers remove Odius and, navigating by observing the progress of military technology, manage to set history straight by dumping him off into the Wild West where a tribe of Native American warriors chase him off into the distance. After that, the travelers return to Dismal's Drug Store. Dismal touches the time machine and disappears, but eventually returns with a pillory. The Stooges manage to remove the pillory with an electric tool.

Back in its heyday, a comedian or comedy team meet picture, was big bucks for any studio. ABBOTT AND COSTELLO MEET FRANKENSTEIN, helped to create this frenzy. Although by the mid-1950s the formula grew stale. Abbott and Costello who had started these meet series were also the ones who eventually destroyed it. But The

Three Stooges had never done a meet picture and the idea seemed like a worthwhile project. It was an immediate success on its initial release! THE THREE STOOGES MEET HERCULES propelled the stooges to dizzying heights in their renewed popularity.

Time travel, ancient Greece, Hercules, monsters and slave ships thrown into a stooge's film created a fast and deliberately slick comedy. The Three Stooges had hit their high Mark! This film set the standards for what was to follow in their next feature film endeavors. Yes, it was a low budget comedy, but it was anything but low budget in producing laughter. The box office receipts proved to Columbia that the stooges were once again a very hot commodity. More movie projects for the stooges were already being drafted. The studio wasn't about to let them go again.

By this time however, The Three Stooges were in demand for just about anything, and they weren't glued to outrageous contract stipulations. Norman Maurer and Moe Howard stirred the team into other avenues as well as continuing to make pictures at Columbia studios.

THE THREE STOOGES IN ORBIT

RELEASED: July, 1962.

RUNNING TIME: 1hour, 27minutes.

DIRECTOR: Edward Bernds.

STUDIO: Columbia.

WITH: Carol Christensen, Edson Stroll, Emil Sitka, George N. Neise, Rayford Barnes, Norman Leavitt, Nestor Paiva,

Don Lamond, Peter Brocco, Thomas Glynn, Jean Charney, Peter Dawson, Maurice Manson, Duane Ament, Bill Dyer, Roy Engel, Jane Wald, Cheerio Meredith and Rusty Wescoatt.

The Three Stooges in Orbit is the fourth feature film to star the Three Stooges after their 1959 resurgence in popularity. By this time, the trio consisted of Moe Howard, Larry Fine, and Joe Derita (dubbed "Curly Joe"). Released by Columbia Pictures, The Three Stooges In Orbit was directed by long-time Stooge director Edward Bernds, who Moe later cited as the team's finest director.

The Stooges are TV actors who are trying to sell ideas for their animated television show The Three Stooges Scrapbook. Unfortunately, their producer does not like anything. He gives the boys ten days to come up with a gimmick or their show will be canceled. In the meantime the Stooges lose their accommodation when they are caught cooking in their room because Curly-Joe turned up the TV-disguised refrigerator way too loud. The only affordable accommodation that will allow cooking is found in an advertisement in a newspaper. The home belongs to Professor Danforth (Emil Sitka) and it resembles a castle.

Professor Danforth is convinced that Martians will soon invade Earth. He persuades the boys to help him with his new military invention—a land, air and sea vehicle (tank, helicopter, flying submarine). In return, Danforth will create a new "electronic animation" machine for the

Stooges to use in their television show. The boys think the Professor a crank but accept his eccentricities along with his accommodation. No one, especially the FBI listens to the Professor's cries for help but the boys apprehend Danforth's butler who dresses like a monster to terrify the Professor. In reality the butler is a Martian spy made to look like a human.

The Martians, meanwhile send two more alien spies named Ogg and Zogg who are not disguised as humans to Earth to prepare for the invasion. When Moe accidentally sends a television transmission of old films and scenes of the Twist craze through the Martian's communication device, they are offended and call off the invasion, opting instead to destroy Earth.

Meanwhile, the Stooges give the vehicle a test run. They mistakenly enter a nuclear test area, when their engine malfunctions. They land near a test rig where a test nuclear depth bomb is set up. The Stooges take the bomb, thinking it is a carburetor, and fasten it to the engine. Water, meant to detonate the bomb, shoots out of the testing rig. The military is bewildered by test's failure. With the bomb attached to the engine, the vehicle now performs beyond expectations, even going into space.

Later, the Martians steal the vehicle, mount a ray gun and begin destroying targets (including Disneyland). The boys sneak onto the craft to stop them. The Stooges are able to use one of the Martians' ray guns to separate the fuselage

151

from the conning tower. The fuselage, holding Ogg and Zogg, crashes into the ocean, detonating the nuclear depth bomb. Clinging to the auto-rotating helicopter section, the Stooges survive, crashing through the roof of their television studio.

THREE STOOGES IN ORBIT is an extension to a failed television pilot, THE THREE STOOGES SCRAPBOOK. Just a slight few notches below HERCULES, it is filled with wild slapstick, verbal puns, and a plot that is simple but very well-orchestrated. The Three Stooges along with Emil Sitka help push the story along from one scene into the next with perfect ease.

Sitka is once again cast as a professor, repeating a similar role he had done so many times when he worked with the stooges over the years in their short two reel comedies during the 40s and 50s. He is an above average supporting character actor who adds the additional needed spice in this movie. He helps the stooges in saving a world that is doomed by invading Martians from Mars. He compliments the stooges and their wild antics naturally.

The scenes where the stooges are trapped either inside or outside the flying submarine are the films greatest highlights. The boys against inanimate objects, gadgets, Martians, all branches of the military and their constant battles between themselves provides a huge variety of clever gags. The added special effects give this film an extra boost!

Another plus, like in the previous feature, the animated opening credits, this early on sets the expected laughs that follow afterward. The film doesn't hesitate in making fun of itself and therefore it is pure comedy from start to finish! A very simple plot device that delivers a huge amount of fast and deliberate action and hilarious minute to minute comedy.

THE THREE STOOGES GO AROUND THE WORLD IN A DAZE

RELEASED: August, 1963.

RUNNING TIME: 1hour, 33minutes.

DIRECTOR: Norman Maurer.

STUDIO: Columbia.

WITH: Jay Sheffield, Joan Freeman, Walter Burke, Peter Forster, Maurice Dallimore, Richard Devon, Anthony Eustrel, Lau Kea, Bob Kino, Phil Arnold, Murray Alper, Don Lamond, Jack Greening, Emil Sitka, Jeffrey Maurer, Audrey Betz, Ramsey Hill, Colin Campbell, Michael St. Clair, Ron Whelan, Kei Chung, John Sheffield, Mark Harris, Aki Aelong, Tom Symonds, Gerald Jann, Laurie Main, Magda Harout, Joe Wong, Harold Fong and Guy Lee.

The Three Stooges Go Around the World in a Daze is the fifth feature film made by The Three Stooges after their 1959 resurgence in popularity. By this time, the trio consisted of Moe Howard, Larry Fine, and Joe Derita (dubbed "Curly Joe"). Directed by Howard's son-in-law Norman Maurer, the film was loosely based on the Jules Verne classic Around the World in Eighty Days.

Phileas Fogg III (Jay Sheffield), great-grandson of the original Phileas Fogg, accepts a bet to duplicate his great-grandfather's famous trip around the world in response to a challenge made by Randolph Stuart III, the descendant of the original Fogg's nemesis. Unbeknownst to anyone, however, "Stuart" is the infamous con man Vicker Cavendish (Peter Forster) who made the bet in order to cover up his robbing the bank of England by framing Fogg for the crime.

With him in this plot is his weaselly Cockney co-conspirator Filch (Walter Burke). This makes for a dangerous journey for Fogg and his servants (the Stooges)

155

and Amelia Carter (Joan Freeman), whom they rescue from thugs during a train ride. On the way, they also: try to steal a cream pie from the galley of a Turkey-bound British cargo ship (and poke the cook in his fat behind with a gaff in the process); watch an elaborate Indian dance at a maharajah's palace, where blind-as-a-bat Curly Joe also regales the maharajah and the viceroy with knife throwing—until his disguise falls off; get captured in China by the Chinese Army, and survive Communist brainwashing in Shanghai with their interrogators turning into Chinese Stooge clones (Moe tells the Chinese general, "No brainee to washee!").

The disgusted Chinese set them adrift in a small boat; use Curly Joe's music-provoked strength to cadge food, clothes, and a trip to San Francisco from the manager of the monstrous sumo Itchy Kitchi (Iau Kea) after a demonstration in a park in Tokyo; stow away in a moving van, supposedly headed for New York. Of course, they are caught, and arrested in Canada by the British inspector (the Stooges and Amelia fake British accents so the inspector will arrest them too).

Back in London, they cross paths again with the two conspirators, again disguised as police—and armed. Of course, the Stooges win out, and, as with the original Phileas Fogg, his descendant miscalculated by one day and still has a chance. Curly Joe gets behind the wheel of the Bobby paddy wagon and speeds across London, and young

Fogg wins the bet—crashing into the Reformer's Club with two seconds to spare.

This is the all-time perfect Three Stooges movie on an epic scale! Next to THE OUTLAWS IS COMING, this film is a joy to watch even if you aren't a stooges fan! Moe's son-in-law, Norman Maurer, takes over directing duties and keeps the laughs, action, adventure, and romance all at a fast and easy flowing movement.

Curly Joe is at his funniest and is given the golden opportunity of taking classic old stooges routines and making them all his own. He incorporates his brand of stooge humor into this fold and comes out looking fresh and funny. He delivers his style of humor in a natural course that helps the movie we are watching flow easily from one scene to the next.

Another important asset in this film is how the stooges' interactions with one another shows that the extreme physical slapstick play among them doesn't have to involve uncomfortable violence. The comic punch of Moe delivering frustrated discipline to his two cohorts is cleverly distributed without having to make a member of the audience watching cringe. This movie has a Disney flavor of humor so familiar at this certain period of time. You don't have to be a stooges fan to enjoy this feature film! It is suitable, a well-executed comedy at its finest.

Unlike the previous Columbia films, which were funny too, this movie is handled in a more delicate sense where it uses the refrained comedy to help the picture to move along. The retelling of the old Jules Verne's story mixed with The Three Stooges wild antics is perfectly blended. It's a shame that SNOW WHITE AND THE THREE STOOGES couldn't have worked in this successful formula. Can you just imagine what that other film would have been like if Norman Maurer had been hired to direct it?

THE OUTLAWS IS COMING

RELEASED: January, 1965

RUNNING TIME: 1hour, 28minutes.

DIRECTOR: Norman Maurer.

STUDIO: Columbia.

WITH: Adam West, Nancy Kovack, Mort Mills, Don Lamond, Rex Holman, Emil Sitka, Henry Gibson, Murray Alper, Tiny Brauer, Marilyn Fox, Sidney Marion, Audrey Betz, Jeffrey Alan Maurer, Lloyd Kino, Paul Frees, Curly-Joe Bolton, Bill Canfield, Hal Fryar, Johnny Ginger, Wayne Mack, Ed T. McDonnell, Bruce Sedley, Paul Shannon and Sally Starr.

The Outlaws Is Coming (stylized as The Outlaws IS Coming!) is the sixth and final theatrical feature film starring The Three Stooges after their 1959 resurgence in popularity. By this time, the trio consisted of Moe Howard, Larry Fine, and Joe Derita (dubbed "Curly Joe"). Like its predecessor, The Three Stooges Go Around the World in a Daze, the film was directed by Moe's son-in-law, Norman Maurer. The supporting cast features a pre-Batman Adam West, Nancy Kovack, and Emil Sitka.

Rance Roden (Don Lamond) plans to kill off all the buffalo and thus cause the Indians to riot. After they destroy the U.S. Cavalry (his real enemy), Rance and his gang will take over the West. Meanwhile, a Boston magazine gets wind of the buffalo slaughter and sends Editor Kenneth Cabot (Adam West) and his associates (Moe, Larry and Curly Joe) to Casper, Wyoming to investigate. Once there, Ken's shooting skills (secretly aided by sharp shooter Annie Oakley (Nancy Kovack)) earn him the job of town sheriff. Rance has his band of bad guys called in to have the lawmen wiped out, but the Stooges sneak into the gang's hideout while the gang is asleep and glue their firearms to their holsters. When Ken confronts the bad guys, the bad guys decide that a life of justice is better than crime. Meanwhile, Rance and Trigger attempt to sell firearms to the Indians, including an armored wagon containing a Gatling Gun and cannon in a turret, but the Stooges foil this plan by snapping a picture of them making the sale.

A good western, whether it be dramatic or comedy has to have atmosphere, this movie has that and lots more! The Three Stooges last theatrical film is a spectacular final showcasing for our boys and a very excellent farewell to a series that spanned almost half a century in entertaining movie going audiences. Not many comedians or comedy teams can boasts such longevity and continued success compared to the stooges and their careers. The Three Stooges out lasted almost everyone! For certain they hold the record for being the longest movie comedy team series.

Not to say that The Three Stooges were finished as a team. For the next five years they were still appearing on television shows, commercials, on stage and doing a series of live action wrap arounds as well as voice overs for their cartoon show. Not to mention mapping out a new television pilot. The Three Stooges even after this movie were still in high demand and their theatrical shorts from the 30s, 40s and 50s would continue to grow in popularity even after they had finally expired with Moe Howard's death in 1975.

THE OUTLAWS IS COMING, had a unique setting, the outlaws casts were actually television hosts who narrated their own independent shows that featured the broadcasting of old Three Stooges short films. It was a great way in saying thank you by the stooges and their personal manager, Norman Maurer. Plus it provided a warm sense of recognizing your favorite city television host throughout the nation. It was also a fantastic marketing tool used to promote this film.

Adam West before he went on to be televisions very first Batman, supports the stooges and his wooden acting is at its superb best! He is the hero who desperately needs heroes to watch over him. The stooges and Nancy Kovack fill that void. Adam West is unaware of the dangers that surround him and he is led to believe that he alone is the sole protector of the depleting buffalo. Ms. Kovack and the stooges in their natural bumbling ways keep one step ahead of West and his inflated ego. Of course his built up ego had inadvertently been constructed by the stooges and Nancy.

Norman Maurer, wrote, produced and directed this bonanza of hilarious Three Stooges antics engulfed in the old west. His personal style along with the stooges give this film a certain, spiced up charm. The supporting players and added character actors all mesh perfectly together and create an enjoyable outing. Once again you don't have to be a diehard stooges fan to enjoy what this movie offers.

KOOK'S TOUR

RELEASED: February, 1970.

RUNNING TIME: 52minutes.

DIRECTOR: Norman Maurer.

STUDIO: United States.

WITH: Moose the dog, Norman Maurer and Jeffrey Maurer.

Kook's Tour is the title of an American short comedy film produced in late 1969 and early 1970. It was the final film to star the Three Stooges and was originally intended as the pilot for a television series. However, on January 9, 1970, before filming was completed, Larry Fine suffered a severe stroke, paralyzing the left side of his body. When it became clear that Fine was not expected to recover fully from the stroke, production of the series was cancelled and the Kook's Tour pilot film was shelved. The film remained unreleased for several years until its director Norman Maurer had the available footage re-edited into a 52-minute presentation and arranged for it to be released to the Super 8 home movie market in the mid-1970s. It has since been released on home video.

The name is a pun on the term "Cook's Tour", which was popularized by the Thomas Cook travel company. This was also a vehicle to show off the great variety of Chrysler Corporation vehicles. All the vehicles shown in this movie were produced by Chrysler, Chrysler RV, and Chrysler Marine Division.

Kook's Tour was the third time the Stooges had tried to create a live-action television series, after their first attempt with Jerks of All Trades in 1949, and then The Three Stooges Scrapbook in 1960.

Following Larry's stroke and the cancellation of Kook's Tour, several attempts were made to revive the Stooges (with Emil Sitka replacing Larry, and Derita attempting to form a new trio for live appearances), but no further films were produced before Larry's and Moe's deaths in 1975 and the final dissolution of the group.

Kook's Tour was conceived by Moe Howard's son-in-law, frequent Three Stooges collaborator Norman Maurer, as a weekly television series that would have mixed the Stooges' brand of farce comedy with a documentary travelogue format. The concept of the series was that, after 50 years of comic mayhem, the Stooges (Moe, Larry Fine and Joe Derita) have retired and are traveling the world with their dog, Moose, motor home, and motor boat (which is transported from place to place via a cargo plane). The 52-minute pilot film for the series saw the Stooges exploring the wilderness of the western United States, including areas of Wyoming and Idaho. In the meantime, Larry keeps getting snubbed when trying to catch a fish and getting a picture of a deer. At the end of the pilot film, Larry, in frustration, throws his hat into the water and fish bite on the fishing hooks attached to it. Larry starts to get excited about catching some fish, but Curly-Joe counts the fish and says "One for me, one for Moe, and one for....Moose!"

The epilogue shows Moe sitting in an office, discussing the trip and stating that their next destination for the second episode (ultimately never produced) was Japan. (Moe makes no reference to Larry's stroke; it's unknown whether this scene was filmed before or after.)

166

The Three Stooges final swan song film was initially released to home theater markets in super8mm. Then in the early 2000's it became available on video and eventually DVD. It has an interesting premise, the stooges are retired performers who decide to take to the road exploring the great open wilderness throughout the United States.

It had been intended as a short series of documentaries showing the beauty and splendor of our great country mixed with the silly antics of the stooges. It is a mildly entertaining program that as time evolves forward becomes more and more of a curiosity of the stooges in their final work as a team than an actual full blown slapstick melee.

It has a much toned down set of stooges. But then again one must remember that the stooges were men now in their late sixties and early seventies. Norman Maurer decided to have a more relaxed style of humor that did away with the wild slapstick of yesteryears. On a whole it isn't a bad film, it works on generating smiles and giggles instead of huge laugh out loud humor. Which is quite understandably reasoned. Had the show worked in its original formatting who knows...it might have created a few more years of The Three Stooges hanging around on our television sets? As it stands today it is a nice piece of added stooges film history for any fan to want to have in their own personal collectable library of Three Stooges memorabilia.

THE END FOLKS!

·

Made in United States
Orlando, FL
27 May 2023

33546219R10093